National Service Fifty Years Ago

Life of a medical conscript in West Africa

NATIONAL SERVICE FIFTY YEARS AGO

LIFE OF A MEDICAL CONSCRIPT IN WEST AFRICA

G C Cook, MD, DSc, FRCP, FRCPE, FRACP, FLS
Visiting Professor, University College London

TROPZAM

Copyright © G C Cook 2014
First published in 2014 by TROPZAM
11 Old London Road, St Albans, Herts, AL1 1QE

Distributed by Gardners Books, 1 Whittle Drive, Eastbourne, East Sussex, BN23 6QH
Tel: +44(0)1323 521555 | Fax: +44(0)1323 521666

www.amolibros.com

The right of G C Cook to be identified as the author of the work has been asserted herein in accordance with the Copyright, Designs and Patents Act 1988.

All rights reserved. This book is sold subject to the condition that it shall not, by way of trade or otherwise, be lent, resold, hired out or otherwise circulated without the publisher's prior consent in any form of binding or cover other than that in which it is published and without a similar condition including this condition being imposed on the subsequent purchaser.

British Library Cataloguing in Publication Data
A catalogue record for this book is available from the British Library.

ISBN 978-0-9560598-3-3

Typeset by Amolibros, Milverton, Somerset
This book production has been managed by Amolibros
Printed and bound by T J International Ltd, Padstow, Cornwall, UK

Contents

List of Illustrations		vi
Preface		xi
Prologue		1
1	'The white man's grave'	9
2	The voyage to West Africa	28
3	Lagos, Nigeria, January–March 1961	37
4	Lagos, Nigeria, April–June 1961	73
5	Lagos, Nigeria, July–September 1961	97
6	Lagos, Nigeria, October–December 1961	112
7	Tour of West Africa: Dahomey, Niger, Togo and Ghana – December 1961	127
8	Lagos, Nigeria, January–March 1962	141
9	Lagos to London	149
10	Epilogue	162
Index		165

List of Illustrations

Fig 0.1: The author's certificate of commission as an officer in the British Army, dated 24th May 1960. 2
Fig 0.2: The 1961 intake into the Royal Army Medical Corps (RAMC), Millbank. 2
Fig 0.3: RAMC Headquarters' Mess, Millbank.. 3
Fig 0.4: Sir James McGrigor (1771-1858), Director-General of the Army Medical Department (1815-51): statue outside the RAMC Mess, Millbank. 4
Fig 0.5: The author's MRCP certificate, dated October 1960. 6
Fig 0.6: Lt-General Sir Robert Drew KBE: Director-General of Army Medical Services in 1961. 7
Fig 1.1: Map of western Nigeria. 10
Fig 1.2: Two Lagos 'night-soil' men photographed in 1961. 24
Fig 2.1: View of Funchal, the capital city of Madeira. 32
Fig 2.2: Lagos Island and its environs – c.1960. 35
Fig 3.1: The Officers' Mess at Yaba. 39
Fig 3.2: Living accommodation at Yaba. 39
Fig 3.3: Captain David Daniels of the Royal Army Dental Corps – a fellow NS conscript (a & b) and mess member. 40
Fig 3.4: Map showing the position of Lagos, and that part of Nigeria which would become familiar to me during fifteen months in West Africa. 43
Fig 3.5: The Federal Palace Hotel, Lagos – probably the best hotel in Nigeria at that time. 45
Fig 3.6: Dr Nnamdi Azikiwe – President of Nigeria in 1961. 45
Fig 3.7: A Royal Nigerian soldier 'on guard'. 46
Fig 3.8: The author in the formal uniform of the Royal Nigerian Army. 46
Fig 3.9: The Military Hospital – Yaba, Lagos. 46
Fig 3.10: My ward sister, a Sierra Leonian. 47

Fig 3.11:	The author dressed in mess kit.	47
Fig 3.12:	Group of Nigerian children in one of the local 'shanty towns'.	48
Fig 3.13:	Street scene in a Lagos 'shanty town'.	48
Fig 3.14:	A view of the Marina, Lagos, which had been established by an early Governor.	49
Fig 3.15:	Ship docked at the Lagos Marina.	49
Fig 3.16:	Carter Bridge, Lagos (named after a former Governor, Sir Gilbert Carter) – a well known 'bottle-neck' for traffic.	49
Fig 3.17:	Example of a Yoruba woman in local dress.	50
Fig 3.18:	Lagos lagoon, viewed from State House.	50
Fig 3.19:	Lagos lagoon.	51
Fig 3.20:	Fishing vessels in the Lagos lagoon.	51
Fig 3.21:	Fishermen on Victoria beach, Lagos.	52
Fig 3.22:	Broad Street, Lagos – viewed from Independence Square.	52
Fig 3.23:	Street scene in urban Lagos.	52
Fig 3.24:	Scene in a Lagos suburb.	53
Fig 3.25:	An example of the Italianate style of building in Lagos.	53
Fig 3.26:	The nineteenth century Anglican cathedral – situated on the Lagos Marina.	54
Fig 3.27:	East End of the Anglican cathedral.	54
Fig 3.28:	Foundation stone laid by Bishop Leslie Gordon Vining, the first Anglican Archbishop of West Africa. (The foundation stone of Bethel Cathedral.)	55
Fig 3.29:	Scene at a race meeting in Lagos.	60
Fig 3.30:	Aerial view of University College Hospital, Ibadan – about ninety miles north-east of Lagos.	60
Fig 3.31:	View of Abeokuta – some sixty miles north of Lagos.	66
Fig 3.32:	Abeokuta market-place.	66
Fig 3.33:	Plaque at the grammar school, Abeokuta.	67
Fig 4.1:	Group of Nigerians in a local village in western Nigeria.	75
Fig 4.2:	Street scene in a rural part of the western region.	75
Fig 4.3:	Group of Nigerians – children and adults in rural Nigeria.	76
Fig 4.4:	Young Nigerian woman in rural Nigeria carrying a large calabash.	76
Fig 4.5:	Group of village-elders in a western Nigerian village.	76
Fig 4.6:	Well-loaded donkey in rural Nigeria.	76
Fig 4.7:	Albino Nigerian boy accompanying a boy with a bicycle. Albinism was not uncommon in the Yoruba population.	78
Fig 4.8:	Local produce at a rural market.	78

Fig 4.9:	Wood carvings at a rural market.	79
Fig 4.10:	An 'alternative medicine' stall at a local market.	79
Fig 4.11:	Native canoe with group of fisherman at Victoria Beach, Lagos.	84
Fig 4.12:	Group of Nigerians on Victoria Beach.	84
Fig 4.13:	Northern Nigerian Muslims with goats about to be 'sacrificed' at the feast of Id-el-Kabir.	87
Fig 4.14:	The River Niger at Jebba.	87
Fig 4.15:	Memorial to Mungo Park and Richard Lander (see text) at Jebba, western Nigeria.	88
Fig 4.16:	Sunrise over the River Niger at Jebba.	88
Fig 5.1:	The author with one of his nursing orderlies at the Military Hospital, Yaba.	103
Fig 5.2	(a and b): Badagri: a favourite venue for a day's outing, usually on a Sunday.	105
Fig 5.3:	Badagri: chains used in the latter years of the 'slave trade'	106
Fig 5.4:	Badagri: photograph of Bishop Crowder, the first Nigerian to be created an Anglican bishop.	106
Fig 5.5:	David Daniels with Jane Garner – a frequent 'fellow' traveller to Badagri. Her father was an army captain, based at Lagos.	107
Fig 5.6:	A Royal Nigerian Army land-rover, with an army driver; the usual form of my transport to Ibadan.	109
Fig 6.1:	Upper-class Moslem resident of Kaduna.	114
Fig 6.2:	Rural scene near Kaduna; this illustrates the usual method of transporting a load in Nigeria.	115
Fig 6.3:	Herd of cattle – near Kaduna.	115
Fig 6.4:	Road sign near Kaduna.	117
Fig 6.5:	Northern camel-rider in ceremonial dress.	117
Fig 6.6:	Zaria: one of the few remaining walled cities in Nigeria.	117
Fig 6.7:	Zaria: the Emir's palace.	117
Fig 6.8	Emir of Zaria in ceremonial dress.	117
Fig 6.9:	Sailing on the Lagos lagoon.	119
Fig 6.10:	Emblem at the entrance to the Lagos museum.	123
Fig 6.11:	Example of Nigerian craftsmanship at the Lagos museum.	123
Fig 6.12:	A Benin bronze artefact at the Lagos museum.	124
Fig 7.1:	Map showing countries of West Africa which were relevant to my December 1961 tour.	128
Fig 7.2:	David Daniels during the West African tour.	129
Fig 7.3:	Example of a laterite road in West Africa.	129

Fig 7.4:	Statue of Kwami Nkrumah in central Accra.	131
Fig 7.5:	Mahogany tree planted by HM Queen Elizabeth II in the Accra Botanical Garden.	131
Fig 7.6:	Accra, Ghana: canoes in the harbour (one of the few on the West Coast) – used for unloading ships.	132
Fig 7.7:	Plaque commemorating the opening of Accra University in November 1959.	132
Fig 7.8:	Hausa horseman in northern Dahomey (now Benin).	135
Fig 7.9:	Tribal dancers in a village in Dahomey.	135
Fig 7.10:	The cathedral at Cotonou, Dahomey.	136
Fig 7.11:	Coastal scene in Dahomey.	136
Fig 7.12:	Village (Ganvie) with a population of 10,000 built entirely on stilts in southern Dahomey.	137
Fig 7.13:	Village scene in Togo.	137
Fig 7.14:	Beach scene at Lomé, the capital of Togo.	138
Fig 8.1:	Official request for a post-mortem examination (subsequently carried out by me) on the body of Albert Ouia.	143
Fig 8.2	(a and b): Cases of smallpox at the Lagos Isolation Hospital.	146
Fig 9.1:	The Via Dolorosa, Jerusalem in the Hashemite Kingdom of Jordan.	151
Fig 9.2:	Street scene in Bethlehem: the Church of the Holy Nativity is in the background.	151
Fig 9.3:	The main square in Cairo, Egypt.	152
Fig 9.4:	One of the Pyramids, Cairo.	152
Fig 9.5:	The Sphinx, Cairo.	153
Fig 9.6:	Scene at Memphis.	154
Fig 9.7:	Exhibits in the Egyptian Museum at Cairo.	154
Fig 9.8:	From the Tutankhamen collection.	155
Fig 9.9:	Tutankhamen's chair, the Egyptian Museum in Cairo.	155
Fig 9.10:	Beirut, Lebanon and the Mediterranean Sea.	157
Fig 9.11:	View in northern Cyprus.	157
Fig 9.12:	Bellapais Abbey, Northern Cyprus.	158
Fig 9.13:	The isle of Poros, Greece.	158
Fig 9.14:	The Vatican, Rome, St Peter's and St Peter's Square.	159
Fig 9.15:	Street scene in Rome.	159
Fig 9.16:	Notre Dame Cathedral, Paris.	160
Fig 9.17:	The Arc de Triomphe, Paris.	160

PREFACE

The major *raison d'etre* of this book is to document nearly fifty letters from West Africa during my period of National Service (NS), a way-of-life which finally came to an end exactly half a century ago. This was an era when the permanent *written word* formed the main medium for most correspondence – long before the rapidly disposable 'e-mail system' came into existence. International communication by telephone was also very far from perfect; even if one could obtain a 'line', which was very expensive, the quality left much to be desired!

I thus began NS in 1960. This was the year in which the British primeminister (Harold Macmillan) made his 'winds of change' speech to the Parliament of South Africa[1], and towards the end of which the landmark trial featuring D H Lawrence's *Lady Chatterley's Lover*[2] took place.

Following the Second World War (1939-45) – a period of great austerity - all British men were compelled to undertake a period of NS in the Navy, Army, or Royal Air Force.[3] As the editor (John Blair) of *The Conscript Doctors: memories of National Service* has emphasised, the NS era (1948-62) was 'unique in British history as [being] the only period [in which] there was conscription in peace time'.[4] This time (which began with eighteen and later became twenty-four months) of full-time service were followed by a spell of four years in the Reserves. It was made *compulsory* (unless one was medically unfit, or rarely, a 'conscientious objector') by Parliament via the National Service Act of 1948, and was justified by, amongst other factors, Churchill's Cold War. The British Army of the Rhine (BAOR) came into effect and the inadequacy of her regular military provision was also highlighted during minor conflicts in Malaya, Korea, Kenya and Cyprus, etc. Most regarded this as being (i) wasteful of time, and (ii) an utter nuisance which interfered with their subsequent (civilian) career. However, many senior UK citizens are convinced that this time spent under rigid military discipline was of value both to the individual in his earlier years, and also to the community at large. It was also frowned upon by and large by 'Regulars' who felt, probably justifiably, that their high standards of training were being undermined by 'amateurs' in their midst.[5] Although the *norm* was to be conscripted immediately after primary and secondary education, those engaged in *medical* courses were granted deferment until *after* qualification, when they were automatically given the King's or Queen's Commission (lieutenant in the first year, and captain in the second). If engaged in higher professional training, they were eligible for added deferment until they had undergone this further course of study.

By far the largest number of conscripts served in Britain. Medical officers (MOs) were largely engaged therefore with the care of basically healthy military personnel and their families or new recruits, so that 'job satisfaction' was low, and many became disillusioned, depressed, and malcontented. Sick parades and examination of prospective recruits also occupied much of the MO's time. Those who applied for a home posting rarely obtained one and vice versa, a fact confirmed in Blair's text. Even if one was favourably treated, the months or days until 'demob' were carefully counted!

This short book also gives an insight into life in Lagos, Nigeria in the immediate post-colonial period. These years were of special relevance to me for, as well as an insight into an unknown environment in the days immediately following 'Empire', they significantly influenced my future career in medicine.[6]

Nineteen sixty-one was an especially interesting year to be living in Nigeria. Independence from colonial rule (and domination) had recently ceased; the position in 1960 (the previous Governor-General had been Sir James Robertson [1899-1983][7]) had suddenly given way to the situation in 1961, when Dr Nnamdi Azikiwe (1904-96)[8] – a Nigerian – was at the helm. The expatriate element, and indeed the entire population was still accustomed to the lifestyle(s) of the British Empire, and although 'independence' had by then become relatively commonplace throughout Africa – following the end of British rule in India in 1947 – the future of Nigeria as an independent, sovereign state had yet to be determined. Viewed retrospectively, the Empire had been both a force for good and ill. The writer, Ben Macintyre recently concluded: 'Only when *imperial* history is divorced from guilt and pride will we be able to see it as it really was, and learn from it.'[9]

I am extremely grateful to my late mother for preservation of correspondence to her (most of it quoted in this book) during my time in West Africa. Although most of the figures are taken from my own photographs, a minority (indicated by an asterisk) are from contemporary picture postcards.

G C Cook
St Albans, June 2012

References and Notes

1. P Catterall (ed). *The Macmillan Diaries II*: 1957-1966. London: Pan; 2012: 265.
2. G H Rolph (ed). *The Trial of Lady Chatterley: Regina v Penguin Books Limited.* London: Penguin Books Ltd 1990: 250; Anonymous. Lady Chatterley's Lover' case opens. *Times,* Lond 1960 ; October 20: 119; Anonymous. End of the Lady Chatterley trial. Ibid November 2: 72.
3. J S G Blair (ed). *The Conscript Doctors: Memories of National Service.* Edinburgh: Pentland Press Ltd 2001: 205; P Doyle, P Evans. National Service. Oxford: Shire Publications Ltd 2012: 64.
4. Ibid (Blair).
5. P Davies. Conscripts who helped to police the Empire. *Times, Lond* 2011: 30 April: 90.
6. G C Cook. *Torrid Disease: Memoirs of a Tropical Physician in the Late Twentieth Century.* St Albans: Tropzam 2011: 93-277.
7. Sir James Robertson (1899-1983). A H M Kirk-Greene. Robertson, Sir James Wilson (1899-1983) In: H C G Matthew, B Harrison (eds). *Oxford Dictionary of National Biography.* Oxford: Oxford University Press 2004 ; 47: 242-4.
8. Nnamdi Azikiwe (1904-96) Anonymous. *Times,* Lond 1996: May 14: 19; A Jackson. Azikiwe, Nnamdi (1904-1996) In: H C G Matthew, B Harrison (eds). *Oxford Dictionary of National Biography.* Oxford: Oxford University Press 2004 ; 3: 66-7.
9. L James. *Raj. the Making and Unmaking of British India.* London: Little, Brown and Co. 1977: 722. L James. *The Illustrated Rise and Fall of the British Empire.* London: Little, Brown and Co. 1999: 352; K Kwarteng. *Ghosts of Empire: Britain's Legacies in the Modern World.* London: Bloomsbury 2011: 465; B Macintyre. What's black and white and red on maps?: anything to do with Empire, it seems. Surely we can both admire the railways and condemn the massacres. *Times, Lond* 2011 ; Nov 29: 25; S Kaur. Historians and the legacy of the Raj. Ibid. 2011 ; Nov 30: 31.

Prologue

In *April 1960*, having avoided conscription for some three years after qualification in medicine (I had undertaken four junior appointments at the Royal Free, Hampstead General [Royal Free Group], Royal Northern and the [Royal] Brompton Hospitals), my period of deferment from National Service (NS) could last no longer and I was compelled to report for a period of two years in the Royal Army Medical Corps (RAMC) (*see* figs 0.1 and 0.2). Two of my maternal uncles had served in the RAMC during the Great War (1914-18) and one had been killed at Loos in 1915; it is of interest that the composer Ralph Vaughan Williams had also served as a private in that corps.[1] After a brief initiation period at Crookham, Surrey into the requirements and demands of an army officer where one learnt a great deal about marching, how to use a rifle, etc, followed by a short course (two weeks) in *tropical medicine* at Millbank – the Headquarters 'Mess' of the RAMC (*see* figs 0.3 and 0.4) – I became a National Service lieutenant. As a commissioned officer, one avoided such unsavoury trivialities as the ceremonial haircut, the use of blanco and 'Brasso', and Kiwi boot polish, but nevertheless failed to escape the administrations of a corporal or more senior non-commissioned officer![2]

One learnt therefore, first and foremost, how to be an 'officer and a gentleman', and there was also time spent 'square-bashing' and teaching on how to use weaponry. However, only a minimal amount of time was devoted to becoming an efficient army doctor.

Service in the Mediterranean area or Middle East were popular postings, while Malaya, Korea, Egypt and the Suez Canal Zone were to be avoided if possible. My initial application for the location of my two years service was for Hong Kong or Singapore, for medicine in the Army 'at home' sounded dull in the extreme (*see* preface). As a result, I was posted initially to Millbank and after a few weeks there, to the Royal Herbert Hospital, Woolwich. Whilst there I was fortunate in passing the examination for Membership of the Royal

Fig 0.3: RAMC Headquarters' Mess, Millbank.

Elizabeth R

Elizabeth the Second by the Grace of God of the United Kingdom of Great Britain and Northern Ireland and of Her other Realms and Territories Queen, Head of the Commonwealth, Defender of the Faith.

To Our Trusty and well beloved Gordon Charles Cook, M.B. Greeting!

We, reposing especial Trust and Confidence in your Loyalty, Courage, and good Conduct, do by these Presents, Constitute and Appoint you to be an Officer in Our Land Forces, from the Second day of May 1960. You are therefore carefully and diligently to discharge your Duty as such in the Rank of Lieutenant or in such other Rank as We may from time to time hereafter be pleased to promote or appoint you to, of which a notification will be made in the London Gazette or in such other manner as may for the time being be prescribed by Us in Council, and you are in such manner and on such occasions as may be prescribed by Us to exercise and well discipline in their duties such officers, men and women as may be placed under your orders from time to time and use your best endeavours to keep them in good order and discipline.

And We do hereby Command them to Obey you as their superior Officer, and you to observe and follow such Orders and Directions as from time to time you shall receive from Us, or any your superior Officer, according to the Rules and Discipline of War, in pursuance of the Trust hereby reposed in you.

Given at Our Court at Saint James's, the Twenty fourth day of May 1960 in the Ninth Year of Our Reign.

Gordon Charles Cook, M.B.

Lieutenant,

Land Forces National Service List

By Her Majesty's Command.

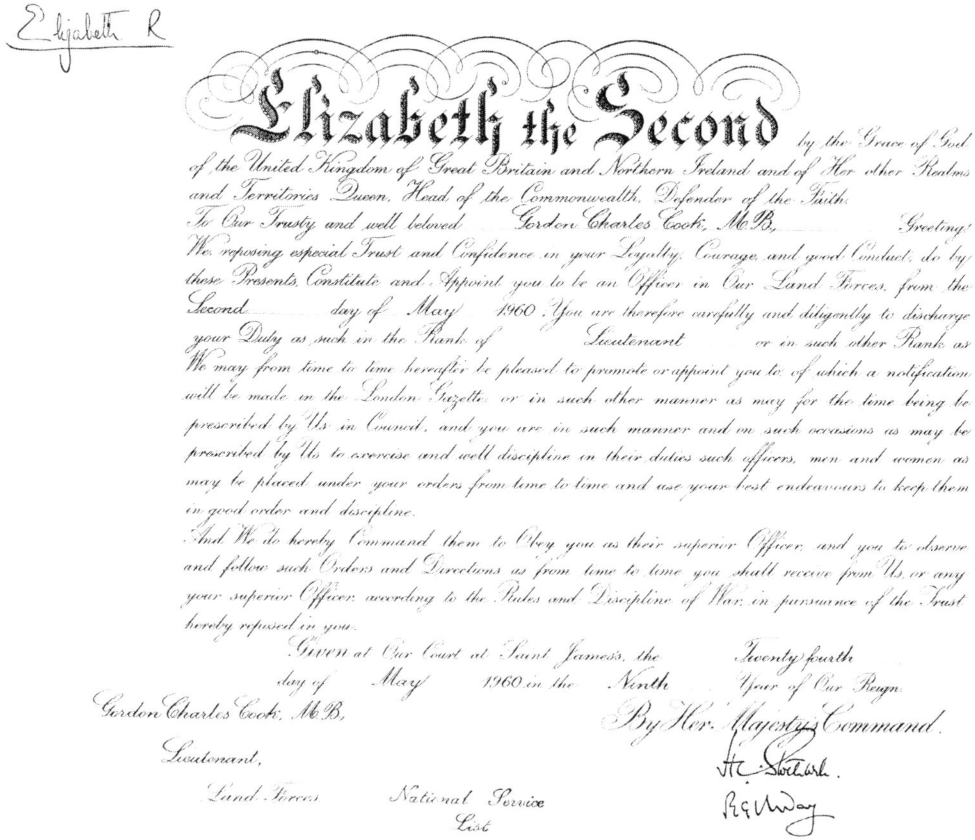

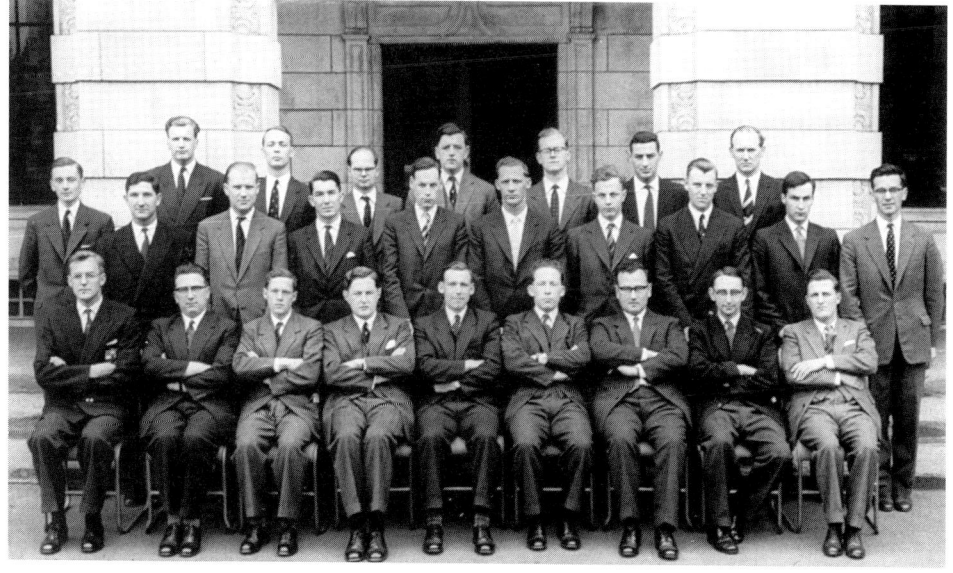

Fig 0.1: The author's certificate of commission as an officer in the British Army, dated 24th May 1960.

Fig 0.2: The 1961 intake into the Royal Army Medical Corps (RAMC), Millbank: the author is fourth from the left, front row.

Fig 0.4: Sir James McGrigor (1771-1858), Director-General of the Army Medical Department (1815-51): statue outside the RAMC Mess, Millbank.

College of Physicians (MRCP) of London (*see* fig 0.5), and having obtained a postgraduate qualification, it was time, I felt, to re-apply for an *overseas* posting. I thus obtained an interview with the Director-General of Army Medical Services – Lieut-General Sir Robert Drew[3] (*see* fig 0.6). He offered either Belfast in Northern Ireland, or if I chose to volunteer, secondment to the Royal Nigerian Army, which had recently been formed as a successor to the Royal West African Frontier Force (RWAFF). I hastily accepted the latter, and after a brief embarkation leave, was offered a passage (at HM Government's expense) by either air or sea to Lagos, Nigeria.[4]

This book therefore provides glimpses of NS life in newly independent Nigeria immediately following independence from British colonial rule, in late 1960. Also, only a little more than half a century of the *new* formal medical speciality *tropical medicine*[5] had by then elapsed; disease in West Africa had been the major catalyst for its launch. The health situation in tropical countries in 1901-2 has been admirably outlined in Dr George Low's correspondence during an expedition to the West Indies.[6]

Sciant Omnes Nos

Robertum Platt, Baronettum Medicinæ Doctorem et Præsidentem Collegii Regalis Medicorum Londinensis, una cum Censoribus, examinásse et approbásse ornatissimum virum, Gordonum Carolum Cook in florentissimá Academiá Londinensi Medicinæ Bacc.^m et cum consensu Sociorum ejusdem Collegii, auctoritate nobis a Domino Rege et Parliamento commissá, ei concessisse has Literas Testimoniales.

In cujus rei fidem et testimonium, adjectis Censorum et Registrarii chirographis, sigillum nostrum commune præsentibus apponi fecimus, datis ex ædibus Collegii die septimo et vicesimo mensis Octobris anno Domini millesimo nongentesimo sexagesimo.

Censoribus,

Registrario,

I certify that _Gordon Charles Cook_ to whom these Letters Testimonial have been granted by the College, and whose signature is subjoined, has been duly admitted a Member of the College.

_____ Member. _____ Assistant-Registrar.

Fig 0.5: *The author's MRCP certificate, dated October 1960.*

Fig 0.6: Lt-General Sir Robert Drew KBE: Director-General of Army Medical Services in 1961.
(Reproduced courtesy the Royal Society of Tropical Medicine and Hygiene.)

References and Notes

1. G C Cook. *Torrid Disease: memoirs of a tropical physician in the late twentieth century.* St Albans: Tropzam 2011: 8; M Hayes. Vaughan Williams: the Christmas-loving agnostic. *BBC Music Mag* 2012; (12): 56-60.
2. J S G Blair. *In arduis fidelis: centenary history of the Royal Army Medical Corps* 1896-1998. Edinburgh: Scottish Academic Press 1998: 564. (*See also*: P Doyle, P Evans. *National Service.* Oxford: Shire Publications Ltd 2012: 62.)
3. **Lt Gen Sir (William) Robert (Macfarlane) Drew** (1907-91) was educated at Sydney Grammar School, Australia, and qualified from Sydney University in 1930. In 1931, he joined the Royal Army Medical Corps (RAMC). During WWII (1939-45) he served in France on the staff of HQ 3rd corps; from 1942-6 he was assistant professor of tropical medicine at the Royal Army Medical (RAM) College. In 1946 he was seconded to Iraq as professor of medicine in the University of Baghdad. Drew returned however, to the RAM College in 1952 as professor of *tropical medicine*. He subsequently became director-general of Army Medical Services. Drew retired from the Army in 1970, and became deputy-director of the British Postgraduate Medical Federation. (*See*: J Baird. *Munk's Roll* II: 1337.)
4. M Crowder. Introduction: *Nigeria 1960.* In: M Crowder (ed). *Nigeria Mag* Lagos: Federal Government Printer 1960 (October): 9-15; M Crowder. Nigeria and its people. *Ibid*: 81-128; T Oloko. *A Tale of 4 Cities* (Lagos, Ibadan, Kaduna and Enugu). *Ibid*: 137-47; U Beier. Oshogbo: Portrait of a Yoruba town. *Ibid*: 148-56; P Verger. Nigeria, Brazil and Cuba. *Ibid*: 167-77; A Euba. Nigerian Music: an appreciation: *Ibid*: 199-208; O Nzekwu (ed). Lagos 1861-1961. *Ibid*: 1961 (August): 91-194. (See also: M Burleigh. *Small Wars, Faraway Places: the Genesis of the Modern World*: 1945-65. London: Macmillan 2013: 588.)
5. G C Cook. *Origin of a Medical Specialty: the Seamen's Hospital Society and Tropical Medicine.* St Albans, Herts: Tropzam 2012: 182.
6. G C Cook. *Caribbean Diseases: Doctor George Low's expedition in 1901-02.* Oxford: Radcliffe Publications 2009: 229; (*See also*: Op cit. See note 5 above.)

1

'The white man's grave'

After I had accepted the RAMC's offer of secondment to the Royal Nigerian Army (RNA), I realised that I knew virtually nothing about Nigeria; indeed, although my knowledge of geography was probably above average (I had passed geography as one of nine school certificate 'O' levels), I am by no means certain that I was even sure of its precise whereabouts on the world map. As for Lagos colony, and the fact that it was formerly one of the largest slave-trading depots in the world, I knew next to nothing. There was, in fact, a great deal to learn!

Nigeria (*see* fig 1.1) simply did not exist before 1860 (a century earlier), but in the mid-*twentieth* century it had the distinction of being the largest possession of the British Crown, and housed one of the most thickly populated areas in Africa. Along the West Coast, populations in former days had fallen into two distinct groups: those on the seaboard were generally small rather inward-looking communities with subsistence economies, whereas those in the northern or *savannah* regions consisted of larger societies with more advanced economies and technology.

At the beginning of the *nineteenth* century it was still not understood that the 'Oil Rivers' formed the delta of the River Niger. In 1830, the Lander brothers in solving this age old puzzle involving the exit of the Niger River, had recorded the whereabouts of the confluence of two great rivers, *i.e.* the Niger and Benue. Although this discovery seemed in theory to 'open up' the interior to European trade, it failed largely for reasons of disease, and it was on this background that regular shipping from Liverpool to the West Coast of Africa began in 1849 (*see* Chapter 2). The confluence of the two rivers was the site which became that of the future Lokoja (the *northern* headquarters of

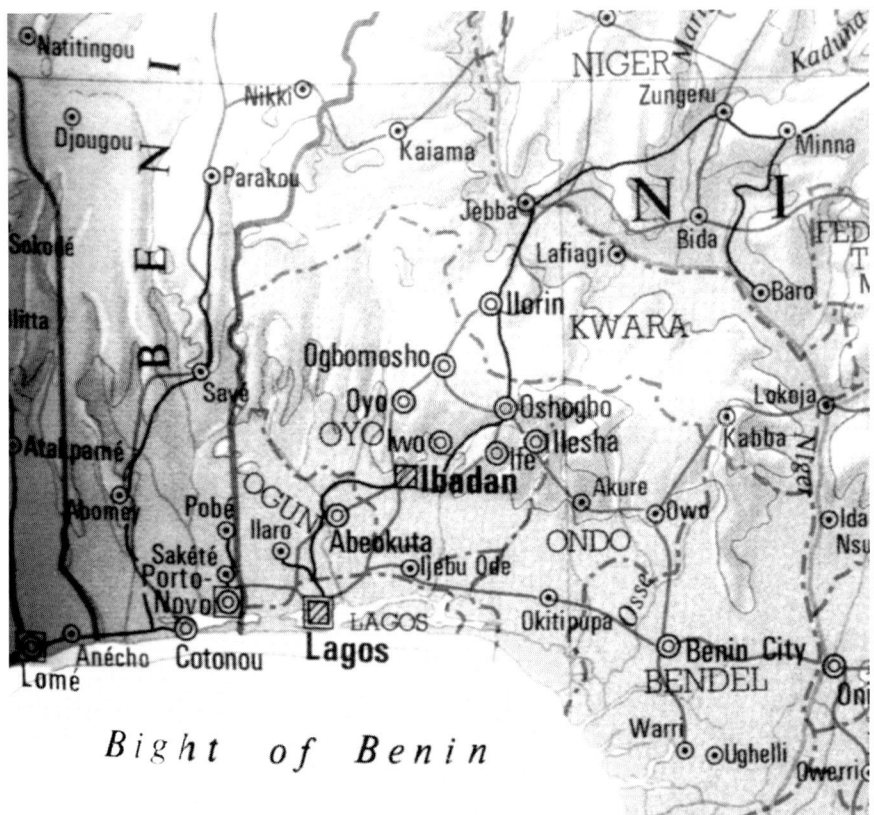

Fig 1.1: Map of western Nigeria. Redrawn from: Anonymous. The Collins World Atlas. London: William Collins and Co Ltd. 1979: 71.

the *Royal Niger Company*, and the main depôt when power was transferred to the Protectorate of *Northern* Nigeria), and where commercial expansion and attempts to eradicate West African slavery emerged. Lokoja was thus the 'germ' of the future Nigeria, and its European settlement was the first on the West Coast, and in fact in the whole of black Africa.

British influence over what is now Nigeria in reality officially occurred in 1843 when Lieutenant John Beecroft (1790-1854) – superintendent of the Naval establishment engaged in suppressing the slave-trade – was based at Santa Isabel (*now* Malabo) on the Spanish island of Fernando Po (*now* Bioko) – 32km off the African coast. Since there was no suitable Spaniard, Beecroft had been appointed acting governor of that island. Six years later he became Consul for the Bights of Biafra and Benin. It was he who took the first step towards the British occupation of Lagos in 1861.

Interest (or lack of it) by the British public of African affairs has been reflected in the literature of the early *nineteenth* century. Charles Dickens (1812-70), the great Victorian novelist, was not alone in being an *antagonist* of these early African crusaders who, he felt, were totally crazy and unnecessary, and he gave the name *Borrioboola-Gha* to the settlement at Lokoja in his novel *Bleak House*, which was to become the focus for this important component of the British Empire.[1] A similar message emerges from *Barnaby Rudge*. This reflects the general opinion of the time, *i.e.*, that the sacrifice of so many lives on the project – aimed at cultivating coffee, educating the natives, and sending out Christian missionaries – was quite unjustified and idealistic.

Today, the *Federal Republic of Nigeria* occupies 923,773 sq km of West Africa. It presently comprises some 250 ethnic groups, of which the Yoruba, Igbo (Ibo), Hausa, and Fulani constitute the major ones. Geographically, Nigeria consists of plateaus, with lowlands (river basins, especially that of the River Niger) between them. Its economy is largely based on petroleum production, and agriculture. The capital city in 1961 was Lagos (*see* below), but since 1991 this has been Abuja – roughly in the *centre* of the country.

Other historical events

Although inhabited for thousands of years, and the centre of the Nok culture from 500 BC until AD 200, it was not until the *fifteenth* century that the country was first visited by Europeans – following which it became a centre of the Atlantic slave-trade (*see* below).

The first contact of Europeans with the West Coast was instigated by Prince Henry of Portugal (1394-1460) whose objective was to find a new route to India. The Gold Coast (*now* Ghana – to the west of Nigeria) was 'discovered' in 1482 and a fort was established at what is now Elmina. It was there and then that a highly lucrative trade in which gold, ivory, pepper, palm oil, ambergris, wax, hides, cotton, rice, millet and wooden bowls were exchanged for cloth, brass bracelets, corals, shells, beads and wine developed.

Until about 1530, the Portuguese had a virtual monopoly of the whole of the West Coast. It was then that the French, followed by the British, became interested and the Atlantic slave-trade developed (*see* below and Chapter 3).

The flag followed trade! The *Royal Niger Company*, whose motto was *Jus, Pax, Ars* which received its royal charter in 1887 and with its headquarters at Asaba, was granted exclusive rights in all those areas of the Niger basin in which it had been trading for many years. The company had a responsibility therefore for administering justice, ensuring peace, eliminating slave-trading, and ending tribal wars. In point of fact, it had a difficult start, not least of involvement in the Battle of Benin. However, its 'up-country' traders did receive support from an unlikely quarter – Mary Kingsley (1862-1900) – for the human virtues which had been to the fore in the slave-trading era, and which persisted in the palm-oil deals. The year before the granting of its royal charter, Britain had declared a protectorate over the whole country ('The Oil Rivers' Protectorate) with its headquarters at Calabar – in the east of present-day Nigeria; the *Royal Niger Company* fell under this protectorate. Sir Claude MacDonald (1852-1915), first Commissioner of the organisation (later the *Niger Coast Protectorate*) was faced with several major problems:

- cannibalism
- murder of twins
- human sacrifice, and
- witchcraft

all of which must have been in existence a century and more before my arrival!

On 1st January 1900, the charter of the *Royal Niger Company* was cancelled, and its territories subsumed by the Imperial Government, while the name of the *Niger Coast Protectorate* was abolished and replaced by *Southern* Nigeria.

In 1914, the Protectorate of *Northern* Nigeria was amalgamated with the Colony and Protectorate of *Southern* Nigeria, under a system introduced by Sir Frederick (later Lord) Lugard (1858-1945), and known as 'Indirect Rule'. When the *Royal Niger Company*'s charter had been revoked fourteen years previously, Britain had assumed direct control over the company's territories north of the Niger, and the *Pax Britannica* was thus slowly spreading over what had formerly been uncivilised territories – which for centuries were *not* subject to strict rule. Although the traditional rulers of the various states had not been deposed, they were joined by advisers in the shape of British residents. The strategy was to leave the native system of law intact while eliminating old cruelties (including slaving), etc. Although this system of 'Indirect Rule' proved eminently successful in Yoruba territory (in the west), this was *not* so in many parts of the east where traditional chiefs were unknown; this part of Nigeria was also far less Christianised than the west, and the power of the ju-ju still reigned supreme! In comparison with the Ibos, the Yorubas were in fact both a civilised and law-abiding community.

The rôle of British administrators in the creation of present-day Nigeria should not be underestimated. Lord Lugard (*see* above) and his wife – Flora Shaw (1852-1929), a prominent journalist – had played an enormously important rôle in the amalgamation of the Yoruba, Ibo, and Hausa dominated regions. A subsequent colonial governor, Sir William MacGregor (1846-1919) (*see* below) invoked tribal chiefs to share in government, and also actively campaigned against disease, especially malaria.

Overall, development of Lagos proceeded well in the years leading to the Great War (1914-18). Following that, developments were relatively slow and few. A serious outbreak of bubonic plague (*Yersinia pestis* infection) in 1924 led to the formation of the *Lagos Executive Development Board* with the clearance of insanitary property over a large area surrounding the Idunmagbo Lagoon. A visit by the Prince of Wales (later King Edward VIII) (1894-1972) in 1925 had caused a stirring of the official conscience.

It is now clear that problems which had bedevilled Nigeria since Lugard's amalgamation in the name of the British Crown had *not* been resolved. Genuine democracy, as Kwarteng has written in 2011, 'is as alien [to Nigerian politicians] as it had been to [George] Goldie [1846-1925] [who pioneered the *Royal Niger Company*], and Lugard at the beginning of the twentieth century'.[2]

Although now the most populous nation on the continent therefore, Nigeria has *not* so far proved to be one of stability; rapid population increase, foreign debt, slow economic growth, a high rate of violent crime and above all, gross government corruption, have all contributed.[3] According to Thorp (*see* above), white men in Nigeria could in days gone by be divided into: traders, missionaries – Mary Slessor (1848-1915) included – and 'warriors', the latter being the latest arrivals.

Trading

Trade between Britain and West Africa, including Nigeria, had its origin in the chartered companies, the most successful of which was the *Royal Africa Company*, which had been founded as long ago as 1672; until the *Company of Merchants Trading to Africa* was founded by Act of Parliament in 1750, trading had been restricted to these companies. Trade was from then 'open' to all British firms. However, trading – which plummeted with the demise of the slave-trade (*see* below) – could not be increased significantly until the interior was safely penetrated, and that could not be achieved until the outlet of the River Niger was discovered (*see* above and Chapter 3).

Little commercial progress was made until the *United Africa Company* (1879) and later the *Royal Niger Company* (1886) came into existence. It was shortly after this that Joseph Chamberlain (1836-1914) entered the scene (*see* below), and in 1900 the *Royal Niger Company* was replaced by the *crown*.

LAGOS (SEE ALSO CHAPTER 3)

Lagos, the capital city in 1961,[4] was of course on the old 'slave coast' which from 1500-1900 constituted the expanse of shore from which about 12 million Africans were shipped to the 'new world', thus forming the Atlantic slave-trade. Slavery was however, restricted to several centres on this coast, of which Lagos and its westerly relation Badagri loomed large. Furthermore, this strip of land was notoriously alien to Europeans. It was not without good reason that a popular jingle arose:

> Beware the Bight of Benin
> for few come out, though many go in!

Sir Harold Scott (1874-1956) has pointed out (*see* below) that so dangerous was the 'West Coast' generally in former times from a disease perspective (he outlined the maladies which the expatriate might encounter) that insurance companies were wary of insuring an individual who was going there. So tedious in fact was life that it was of little surprise that so many 'west coasters' took to 'cards and drink'; it was 'A land of plague and pestilence...where ju-ju and superstition reigned'.

Scott has also written:

> Under British rule Lagos [later] attained in spite of its climate of ill repute and of the loss by invaliding and death of [numerous] officials, remarkable prosperity; in fact, because of the commercial activity of the port, it was [often] spoken of as the Liverpool of West Africa.

He continued:

> Three forces were [as late as] 1939, at work, [the first] two beneficial and [the third] the opposite': ... [*first*] the *Niger Coast Protectorate* – to keep trade routes open, and suppress bloodshed and sacrifice, [*second*] the *Royal Niger Company* – centred on administration of trade over extensive areas, and...*third*, Ju-ju, the power behind the throne in much of West Africa.[5]

Later events in Nigeria

During and before World War II (1939-45), southerners such as Nnamdi Azikiwe (1904-96) (*see* below) were already involved in the Nigerian independence movement, while others (including many Yoruba chiefs) appreciated that they 'had something to lose from the demise of Empire'. The preservation of British values (as laid down by Lugard) was ardently defended by the Islamic northerners such as the Sardauna of Sokoto (educated in *northern* Nigeria on English lines). However, in the aftermath of WWII, and hastened by the Indian example of 1947, independence became a 'foregone conclusion', although there remained a deal of conservative dominance in the north (much championed by the Sardauna himself). In late 1960 (immediately before my arrival there), Nigeria had in fact become independent, and three years later was made a republic.

Following 'independence' (*see* above), the *northerners* and Igbos (in the east of the country) amalgamated and in effect dominated the more 'western educated' Yorubas for a short time. By 1962, the north (headed by the Sardauna, and his henchman Balewa – now the Federal Prime Minister [*see* below]) – attempted to dominate the west and east, politically. This ultimately resulted in the Biafran War (*see* below), with the shooting and death of the Sardauna by eastern soldiers; meanwhile, Balewa and Akintola (premier of the western region) were also killed. However, the British Government continued to support the Federal Government – which it had created – and under no circumstance would it recognise a separate 'oil-rich' Eastern state. Despite that strategy, the 'Republic of Biafra' was born, largely as a result of the foundation of a separate Ibo state led by C M Ojukwu (1933-2011); a sharp division came about between the east and north. This conflict, which lasted nearly three years, produced a temporary famine and was accompanied by a humanitarian crisis. The Biafrans subsequently surrendered. Overall the war achieved little apart from creating a greater awareness of tribal and family connections, and it also resulted in increased tensions between Nigeria's Christians and Muslims.[6] By 1967 (long after my departure), Nigeria was in a state of serious crisis, which had resulted in a civil war and the death of one million easterners (Biafrans).

A recent report on developments in industry, business and the national economy shows Nigeria in a far more encouraging light.[7]

Disease on the 'West Coast'

There can be little doubt that *yellow fever* ('yellow jack') and *malaria* have been the two most feared diseases in the 'white man's grave'; these carried the highest mortality rates, especially amongst new arrivals. Coupled with the 'fever' however, was dysentery – both amoebic and bacillary. Inadequate sanitation continued to be a problem in 1961 in most of Nigeria – especially in urban conurbations, where daily collections of 'night soil' were all too apparent.

Bonny on the Niger delta, was notoriously bad for disease – in particular *yellow fever* – when in the late *nineteenth* century, according to Thorp (*see* above), the trader's agent was often based on an old hulk moored off the coast. In the early *twentieth* century, as trading moved inland (drinking-water was often taken straight from a river), the situation regarding disease failed to improve.

The situation in Sierra Leone (to the west of Nigeria) in 1803 has been admirably summarised by Thomas Winterbottom (1766-1859)[8], and more recently Howard Petraza (*see* above) has related the enormous mortality on the first voyages of exploration to Nigeria – which had trade as its major *raison d'etre* – to the River Niger, and the Benue in 1832. James Boyle (? – 1862) MRCS, a colonial surgeon in Sierra Leone, gave in 1831 what is probably the first accurate medical account of 'West Coast fevers': *A Practical Medico-Historical Account of the Western Coast of Africa* (1831). He regarded Accra as the healthiest spot on the coast on account of its 'open hinterland'; otherwise, the Gold Coast (*now* Ghana) was 'the most unfriendly [location] to man on the face of the globe'. Most disease, he considered, arose from miasmata rising from the swamps. Another version of the popular jingle of the time has been given by Lloyd and Coulter:

Beware and take care of the Bight of Benin.
There's one comes out for forty goes in.

In order to suppress the slave-trade (*see* below), which had been officially abolished in 1807, but which was to continue illegitimately, in the hands of the Portuguese using American vessels until 1865, Britain maintained a squadron of small ships (the anti-slavery patrol) on the West coast – undoubtedly the 'most unhealthy part of the world' – associated with the prevailing miasmatic theory of 'fevers'. The oldest slaving rivers were: the Bonny, Calabar, Cameroons, and the 'Oil Rivers' (all branches of the Niger). The position regarding expatriates in the mid-*nineteenth* century from a disease perspective has also been admirably set out by Lloyd and Coulter, who began their chapter entitled 'The West African Squadron':

> Dr Alexander Bryson (1802-69) called the ... Squadron [in 1847] 'the most disagreeable, arduous and unhealthy service that falls to the lot of British officers and seamen ...'[9]

The slave-traders (*see* below) operated over a total of 3,000 miles of coast – from the Gambia (in the north) to the mouth of the Congo. The great rivers, emerging at the Niger delta were then too malarious to attract legitimate traders. Meanwhile, a few white settlers occupied a handful of forts and factories along the Gulf of Guinea. At the colonial port of Freetown (Sierra Leone), for example, ships could only remain at anchor for a few days without putting their crews at serious risk from one of the fevers, including *malaria, yellow fever* and *'blackwater'*. Even as late as the 1870s, shipping companies apparently refused to issue return tickets to the Niger! Lloyd and Coulter (*see* above) gave numerous examples of the vast mortality on naval vessels; the further up the West African rivers they sailed, the greater was the mortality-rate from both *malaria* and *yellow fever*.[10]

Plasmodium falciparum Malaria

Until Alphonse Laveran (1845-1922)'s work, which had demonstrated the causative agent of malaria (*Plasmodium* spp infection), it was of course impossible to differentiate beyond doubt the true identity of a presumed malarial infection. This disease was therefore at that time virtually impossible to separate from other fevers (especially *yellow fever* – see below). That the malignant form of the infection, caused by *P falciparum*, was commonplace throughout West Africa from time immemorial is undisputed. Thus, in the *nineteenth* century this disease formed a major health hazard, particularly in the non-immune. In 1897-8, Sir Ronald Ross (1857-1932) FRS confirmed mosquito transmission of the disease in India. However, prevention still relied very largely, as it had done for nearly three centuries, on 'the bark' or quinine. It was not until the 1930s that synthetic anti-malarial agents became available. Thus, by the 1960s (when I was in Lagos), prophylaxis was centred on proguanil ('Paludrine'), taken orally daily (*see* Chapter 3). This was *before* the days of multiply 'resistant' strains of *P falciparum*.[11]

Yellow fever (the 'black vomit')

In early reports, 'yellow jack' was considered to be a 'climatic disease', and differentiation from malaria was difficult or often impossible. Furthermore, it was incurable, quinine or 'the bark' being ineffective. Whereas venesection was sometimes of value in malaria, this procedure was potentially fatal in *yellow fever*. Many authors stressed the 'highly infectious character' of *yellow fever* (see below). According to Fowler and his colleagues, writing in 1914, *yellow fever* had been endemic in West Africa since around 1500; it had certainly been present 'on the adjacent islands or…the mainland of the West African coast during the *sixteenth* and *seventeenth* centuries…'. A severe epidemic 'throughout European settlements on the Coast' arose between 1823 and 25. In Nigeria, the disease, often epidemic, had caused a significant mortality-rate throughout the country during the *nineteenth* century. These authors concluded that:

> …there is no [historical] evidence to shew that the infection [had ever] been introduced from outside Africa.[12]

Lloyd and Coulter (*see* above) concluded that: 'More information regarding *yellow fever* in the *nineteenth* century is to be found in the journals of naval and military surgeons than anywhere else.' They cite the view that this disease, although not then considered contagious, originated in the interior of Africa, *e.g.* at 'the Ibadan focus'.

It was not, however, until the turn of the century that mosquito transmission had been clearly established by Major Walter Reed's (1851-1902) medical team in Cuba, although the physician Carlos Finlay (1833-1915) had suggested this as early as 1881. Regarding the causative agent, attempts to incriminate various bacteria commenced as far back as 1888, the most favoured culprit originally being a spirochaete identified by the Japanese investigator Hideyo Noguchi (1876-1928) in 1919. Another alleged causative agent – *Leptospira icterohaemorrhagiae* – ultimately transpired to be the cause of Weil's disease. Noguchi later maintained that *L icteroides* (which was in fact probably also *L icterohaemorrhagiae*) was responsible for the disease in South America; however, in attempting to establish this association at Yaba – a suburb of Lagos – in 1928, he himself developed *yellow fever* and died shortly afterwards at Accra, Ghana. An Irish investigator, Adrian Stokes (1887-1927) had died of *yellow fever* while investigating the disease at Yaba the previous year; these discoveries however, paved the way for proof of the viral origin of this disease – which led to effective immunisation – in the early 1930s. In 1951, a South African, Max Theiler (1899-1972) received the Nobel Prize in physiology or medicine for developing the 17D vaccine.[13]

The disease spectrum on the west coast of Africa during World War II has been summarised by both R M Murray-Lyon[14] and J S K Boyd.[15] It emerged that a wide range of entities, apart from *malaria* and *yellow fever*, – from viral diseases to west African trypanosomiasis and sickle-cell disease – were involved.[16]

Summarising living conditions in West Africa today, it is not the heat or disease, but high humidity, both day and night, persisting most of the year, which becomes extremely tiresome. From a disease perspective there is little for the present-day expatriate to fear; although mild gastrointestinal infections are commonplace, major health problems are, hopefully, a thing of the past. I would conclude however, that if you can survive a 'tour' of coastal West Africa even today, you can probably stand anything! This, I was soon to find out at first hand.

The Atlantic slave-trade

In the early *fifteenth* century, Europeans (Portuguese) had been attracted for the first time to West Africa (*see* above); although their primary aim was to seek new resources, they began by bringing gold, ivory and African slaves to Europe, and seeking new trade routes to south-east Asia. The potential for exploitation of the *human* resource was not, however, fully appreciated until the discovery of America in 1492, with a consequent demand for labour to work in the plantations – set up for the growing of cotton, tobacco, coffee, sugar cane, cocoa and rice. Thus, the Atlantic slave-trade began, and Britain was to become largely instrumental in both its dominance, and incidentally also its later abolition (*see* below).

Slavery *within* Africa was of course nothing new (*see* above), but orientation towards the *Atlantic* trade, was a novel and unique phenomenon. It was on this background that the 'triangular trade' developed. Captured Africans (some had been sold by their communities) endured a forced march to the 'slave-coast' (*see* above), and were often accommodated in a fort (*see* Chapter 7), from which they were transported to America (the 'Middle Passage') in appalling conditions. Ships involved in this industry arrived from Europe after having transported, amongst other items, guns, gunpowder and alcohol to Africa; in addition they contained a few passengers to man the coastal forts – many managed by the *Royal African Company* – and also the administrative centres. The ships taking the slaves to America (*see* Chapter 2) were also loaded with gold and ivory – most eventually to end up in Europe – together with African cloth and metalwork to be sold in the Caribbean islands, or possibly Europe. The final (third) leg in the 'triangular-trade' was designed to transport local produce – sugar, coffee, cocoa, cotton, rice and tobacco – from the Americas (including the Caribbean) to Europe. Most captured Africans, on arrival in the Americas (including the Caribbean), would be auctioned at a 'slave-market' under humiliating conditions. Not all would, however, end up in plantations; some would be destined to become domestic servants.

Many plantation owners spent little or no time in the Americas, but simply accepted their profits, which they used to build mansions, etc in Britain. Most importation of Africans into the Americas (most to the 'deep South' or the Caribbean) ceased in 1807, *i.e.* when Britain declared the trade to be illegal; however, it continued for various lengths of time in vessels owned by other nations.

It is of interest to recall that when the *Seamen's Hospital Society* (SHS) – later to establish *tropical medicine* as a formal discipline – was established in 1821, the slave-trade was still much in evidence.[17] Perhaps the most visible evidence of the slave-trade in Lagos today is to be found in the major square – *Tinubu Square*. Madam Tinubu had in the 1850s and '60s (and probably before that) been associated with the trade, from which she had accumulated significant profits. She proved to be a 'thorn in the flesh' to those working to suppress the trade, and hatched plots to expel the British, including the governor of the day – Benjamin Campbell – from Lagos, and furthermore to plunder their warehouses. In fact, she attempted to re-establish the trade.

As the slave-trade slowed, traders switched to *palm oil* (*see* above), which with the Industrial Revolution in full swing in England, was in great demand. In the latter days of the *nineteenth* century, this commodity would therefore be exchanged for: cotton, iron bars, and manillas (many of them manufactured in Birmingham – *see* Chapter 3), etc.

THE ANTI-SLAVERY MOVEMENT

The anti-slavery movement is likewise of interest. George Fox (1624-91), an English Dissenter and founder of the Quaker sect (the Society of Friends) in the *seventeenth* century, was unhappy with the way in which plantation owners treated their slaves, but it was two Anglicans, Granville Sharp and Thomas Clarkson (with William Wilberforce MP as their parliamentary spokesman) who initiated the abolitionist movement, the *Anti-Slavery Society* being founded in 1823. The formation of the puritanical Quakers at this time, before Anglicanism took hold, is not without interest. As early as 1787, British abolitionists had inaugurated Freetown in Sierra Leone to receive: (i) repatriated and 'rescued' Africans, and (ii) those in domestic service in London. The 'West African Squadron' (*see* above) had been set up by the Royal Navy in 1808 to patrol the Bights (including major rivers), and to carry out a watch for slavers. Between 1808 and 88, it is estimated that British naval patrols freed 150,000 African slaves from about 1,600 slave ships – most ending up in Freetown.

In 1833, despite a great deal of opposition from those who had vested interests in American plantations, the British Government passed a Bill, which became law on 1st August 1834, outlawing slavery in every *British* territory, and as a result slave owners received £20 million in compensation, *i.e.* £12 per slave. However, this by no means heralded the end of slavery, which still existed in other countries, and the *British and Foreign Anti-Slavery Society* was hence founded in 1839. Despite this, according to Thorp (*see* above), Lagos was still 'full of slave traders [as late as 1852]: Brazilian, Spanish, Portuguese, French, and possibly even an occasional Briton'. The following year she wrote, 'trees [were still] covered with human skulls', indicating that Lagosians 'had not abandoned their [other] unsavoury practices' either.[18]

Although in the mid-*nineteenth* century, coastal regions were still dominated by trading (slavery was at that time slowly giving way to palm-oil as the principal export – *see* above) in the interior, in for example Abeokuta and Ibadan, missionaries by then held sway.

In the USA, the Quakers also took up the cudgels early on and the trade there had been made illegal in 1808, the colony of Liberia being later established in 1821-2 for the reception of '*free* slaves'. By the 1830s there had been a great deal of unsuccessful pressure by the USA on the southern American states, and although Pope Gregory XVI condemned slavery in 1839, the Roman Catholic church (especially that in Ireland) remained ambivalent. It thus took very many years for the trade to finally disappear. It was not, until 1865 (at the end of the civil war in the USA) that, under Abraham Lincoln (1809-65), slavery was *officially* stamped out.

Aftermath of the trade

As Sadler has pointed out in his very readable book, the slave-trade left several important legacies. Racism, *i.e.* the proposition that white skins are superior to black, became a concept of the past. Women's suffrage was also given a boost. In the field of architecture, many extant buildings are either reminders of feuding arising from the trade, or they remain relics of it. The Industrial

Revolution, and hence the British Empire, was rendered possible by profits from the trade. The origin(s) of many banking and insurance institutions can be traced to the trade, and statues of many philanthropists who helped abolish slavery remain extant. Numerous present-day cultural activities in Europe and the Americas – including music, literature, and art – have been enriched by slavery, and certain sects of Christianity – especially those of the Methodists and Baptists – were boosted by the trade.[19]

Joseph Chamberlain (1836-1914) and 'constructive imperialism'

Throughout history therefore, West Africa – especially the 'Bight of Benin' – had presented a hostile environment for non-immunes, and that almost always applied to the white man. Towards the end of the *nineteenth* century, it became abundantly clear to the Secretary of State for the Colonies (Joseph Chamberlain) that something had to be done from a health perspective for the servants of Empire, for above all, morbidity and mortality amongst Colonial servants in West Africa was unacceptably high. What therefore was to be done?

Chamberlain was at that time aware that Doctor (later Sir) Patrick Manson (1844-1922),[20] recently returned from China, was giving lectures in London – notably at St George's Hospital and Livingstone College (a missionary organisation) – on *tropical medicine*. He thus felt that Colonial Medical Officers, especially those from West Africa, when on furlough, should attend these. In July 1897, he therefore created Manson the Medical Adviser to the Colonial Office. Their joint collaboration gave birth (following various controversies) to the *London School of Tropical Medicine* (LSTM) at the Albert Dock Hospital under the auspices of the SHS (*see* above).[21] Special education in *tropical medicine* (Manson's dream) had thus materialised. Colonisation of West Africa with attention to the health of officials and agents of commerce would, it was envisaged, be taken care of and this was destined to improve in future years. As a result, the 'White Man's Grave' was converted into a far more tolerable posting. There would also be a West African Medical Service with higher rates of pay to its medical staff than had formerly been the case.

It was on this background that the *Liverpool School of Tropical Medicine* and to a far lesser extent, the LSTM launched expeditions to Nigeria, the Gambia and other West African countries. The objects of Liverpool's expedition to Nigeria in 1900 for example, the members of which were: H E Annett, J E Dutton and J H Elliott, and was to last seven months, were:

- to further explore West Africa to ascertain under what varied conditions mosquitoes of the genus *Anopheles* lived and propagated, with a view of ascertaining the most feasible and practical methods of preventing malarial fever,

- to investigate the conditions under which malarial fever is conveyed to Europeans, [and]
- to corroborate and extend recent discoveries *i.e.* those of Ross, and researches on the subject.

The remit of this expedition was also to study 'other tropical diseases as opportunity arose, and to note…the general sanitation condition of the places visited'. Reports relating to the Liverpool expeditions were published as 'Memoirs' by the *Liverpool School of Tropical Medicine*.[22]

Nigeria in 1961

Problems associated with the Lagos Bar – a shipping hazard (*see* Chapter 3) – had by 1917 been laid to rest. By the 1950s, with the 1939-45 world war rapidly fading into past memory, religion and morals – which had dominated the scenario in the early days of the *twentieth* century – closely followed by economics, had been replaced by *politics* and also the race for independence from colonial rule. The lone trader of the 1850s had given way to the comfortably living businessman of the 1960s. Instead of having to attend law and medicine courses in British universities, young Nigerians could now graduate in their own country. Women in Nigeria still however carried their picaninnies (babies) on their backs, and most loads were still confined to the head! Although *nineteenth* century health hazards had by 1961 been largely circumvented (Lagos for example, had had a piped water-supply since 1916, replacing numerous wells – most of which had been heavily contaminated), the 'night-soil' men (*see* fig 1.2) still existed. 'Mammy wagons' still transported the less wealthy in urban and rural areas alike.

The Nigeria which I was to enter in 1961 therefore sounded unrecognisable from that in historical accounts. Or was it? Certainly things on the surface seemed very different, but had the infra-structure of society really changed? I was shortly to find out.

Fig 1.2: Two Lagos 'night-soil' men photographed in 1961.

References and notes

1. H J Pedraza. *Borrioboola-Gha: the story of Lokoja, the first British Settlement in Nigeria.* London: Oxford University Press 1960: 118.
2. K Kwarteng. *Ghosts of Empire: Britain's legacies in the modern world.* London: Bloomsbury 2011: 298-323.
3. E Thorp. *Ladder of Bones.* London: Jonathan Cape 1956: 320; R Collis. *A doctor's Nigeria.* London: Secker and Wärburg 1960: 264; T Hodgkin. *Nigerian perspectives: an historical anthology* 2nd ed. London: Oxford University Press 1975: 432. [See also: M Perham. Lugard. *Nigeria Magazine* 1960 (October): 46-52; S de Gramont. *The Strong Brown God: the story of the Niger River.* London: Hart Davis, MacGibbon 1975: 350; A H M Kirk-Greene. Lugard, Frederick John Dealtry, Baron Lugard (1858-1945). In: H C G Matthew, B Harrison (eds). *Oxford Dictionary of National Biography.* Oxford: Oxford University Press 2004; 34: 727-33; F P Sprent, L Milne, MacGregor, Sir William (1846-1929). In: H C G Matthew, B Harrison (eds). *Oxford Dictionary of National Biography.* Oxford: Oxford University Press 2004; 35: 444-5; Op cit. See note 1 above.
4. Op cit. See note 3 above (Thorp); I Ryan. *Black Man's Palavar.* London: Jonathan Cape 1958: 252; M Crowder (ed). *Nigeria Mag: Lagos Centenary Supplement* 1960 (August): 91-194.)
5. H H Scott. *A history of tropical medicine.* London: Arnold (2 vols) 1939: 68-79.
6. Anonymous. Nigeria: *officially* the Federal Republic of Nigeria. *Britannica Concise Encyclopedia.* London: Encyclopedia Britannia, Inc. 2002: 1327-8; F Forsyth. *The making of an African legend; the Biafra story.* London: Severn House Publishers Ltd 1983: 288; Anonymous. Chukwuemeka Odumegwu Ojukwu: Nigerian soldier who in 1967 led the Ibo people in the breakaway republic of Biafra that ended in widespread killings and starvation. *Times, Lond* 2011: Nov 28: 49.
7. Upper Reach. Nigeria: a paradigm shift in West Africa. *Times, Lond* (suppl). 2012; Dec 10: 1-28.
8. T Winterbottom. *An account of the Native Africans in the neighbourhood of Sierra Leone to which is added an account of the present state of medicine among them.* 2nd ed. London: Frank Cass & Co Ltd 1969; ii: 13-31; Op cit. See note 1 above.
9. A Bryson. *Report on the Climate and Principal Diseases of the African*

Station; compiled from documents in the office of the Director-General of the Medical Department, and from other sources. London: William Clowes and Sons 1847: 266; C Lloyd, J L S Coulter. The West African squadron. In: *Medicine and the Navy 1200-1900.* London: E & S Livingstone Ltd 1963; 4: 155-72. [*See also*: A Bryson. *Account of the Epidemic Fever of Sierra Leone* 1849: 33; J Boyle. *A Practical Medico-Historical Account of the Western Coast of Africa.* 1931]. **Alexander Bryson** was originally a surgeon on the West Africa Squadron who eventually became Director General of the Naval Medical Service. His report of 1849 is felt to be more reliable than government statistics of the time, and his use of quinine in prevention and cure of malaria is considered to have significantly reduced the impact of malaria on the squadron.

10. Ibid.
11. C Singer, E A Underwood. *A Short History of Medicine.* 2nd ed, Oxford: Clarendon Press: 454-66; G C Cook. *Tropical Medicine: an illustrated history of the pioneers.* London: Academic Press 2007: 67-102; W F Bynum. Ross, Sir Ronald (1857-1932). In: H C G Matthew, B Harrison (eds). *Oxford Dictionary of National Biography.* Oxford: Oxford University Press 2004; 47: 842-6. (*See also*: N J White. Malaria. In: G C Cook, A I Zumla (eds). *Manson's Tropical Diseases* 22nd ed. Saunders/Elsevier 2003: 1201-1300.)
12. J K Fowler, W J Simpson, R Ross, W B Leishman. *Yellow Fever Commission (West Africa).* 2nd report 1914: 147.
13. Op cit. See Note 11 (Singer, Underwood: 466-81; Cook: 103-13) above. [*See also*: (J T W). Adrian Stokes 1887-1927. *J Path Bact* 1928; 31: 121-5; G Eckstein. *Noguchi.* London: Harper and Brother Publishers 1931: 419; M Elliott. Yellow fever in the recently inoculated. *Trans R Soc Trop Med Hyg* 1944-5; 38: 231-4; B Maegraith. Yellow fever in West Africa. Ibid 1945-6; 39: 347-8; G Williams. *The plague killers.* New York: Charles Scribner's Sons 1969: 345; Anonymous. *Prevention and Control of Yellow Fever in Africa.* Geneva: WHO 1986; D W Smith, R A Hall, C A Johansen, A K Broom, J S Mackenzie. Yellow fever virus. In: G C Cook, A I Zumla (eds). *Manson's Tropical Diseases.* 22nd end. Saunders/Elsevier 2003: 742-5.]
14. **Ranald Malcolm Murray-Lyon** qualified (MB, ChB) from Edinburgh in 1926, and proceeded to the MD three years later. He was elected FRCPE in 1933. Following several junior appointments in Scotland, he joined the RAMC, in which he became a Lt-Colonel. During WWII, he served in the Gambia. (*See*: Anonymous. *Medical Directory 1950*: London J & A Churchill: 563.)

15. **Sir John Boyd** qualified from Glasgow University in 1913. After service in the RAMC at Ypres and Salonica in the Great War (1914-18), he specialised in bacteriology. He later served in India where he reached the rank of Brigadier. Boyd subsequently became Director of Pathology at the War Office, and Director of the Wellcome Laboratories of Tropical Medicine. He was an authority on shigellosis. (*See*: P O Williams. Boyd, Sir John Smith Knox [1891-1981]. In: H C G Matthew, B Harrison (eds). *Oxford Dictionary of National Biography.* Oxford: Oxford University Press 2004; 7: 39- .)
16. R M Murray-Lyon. Important diseases affecting West African native troops. *Trans R Soc Trop Med Hyg* 1944; 37: 287-302; J S K Boyd. Advances in tropical medicine. In: V Z Cope. *History of the Second World War: Medicine and Pathology.* London: H M Stationery Office 1952: 195-221.
17. H Jacobs. *Incidents in the Life of a Slave Girl.* London: Penguin Books 2000: 277; G C Cook. *History of the Seamen's Hospital Society. J Greenwich Hist Soc* 2005; 3(2): 67-78; Op cit. See note 11 (Cook 2007) above.
18. Op cit. See note 3 (Thorp) above: 46. [*See also*: H B Stowe. *Uncle Tom's Cabin or Life among the Lowly.* London: Penguin. 1986: 629; R Smith. Learning from the abolitionists, the first social movement. *Br Med J* 2012; 345: 56-8].
19. H Thomas. *The Slave Trade: the History of the Atlantic Slave Trade 1440-1870.* London: Picador 1997: 925. [*See also*: N Sadler. *The Slave Trade.* Oxford: Shire Publications Ltd 2009: 64; J Walvin. *The Slave Trade.* London: Thames and Hudson 2011: 144].
20. P H Manson-Bahr, A Alcock. *The Life and Work of Sir Patrick Manson.* London: Cassell and Co Ltd 1927: 104-20.
21. G C Cook. Doctor Patrick Manson's leading opposition in the establishment of the London School of Tropical Medicine: Curnow, Anderson, and Turner. *J Med Biog* 1995; 3: 170-7; G C Cook. *From the Greenwich Hulks to Old St Pancras: a History of Tropical Disease in London.* London: Athlone Press 1992: 147-62; G C Cook. *Disease in the Merchant Navy: a History of the Seamen's Hospital Society.* Oxford: Radcliffe Publishing Ltd 2007: 415-34; G C Cook. *Origin of a Medical Specialty: the Seamen's Hospital Society and Tropical Medicine.* St Albans: Tropzam 2012: 182.
22. Anonymous. *Report of the Malaria Expedition to Nigeria of the Liverpool School of Tropical Medicine and Medical Parasitology … .* Liverpool: University Press 1901: 68; Anonymous. *Report of the Malaria Expedition to the Gambia 1902 of the Liverpool School of Tropical Medicine and Medical Parasitology.* London: Longmans, Green & Co 1903: 46.

2

The voyage to West Africa

As well as a short embarkation leave, I was offered either a sea or air passage to Nigeria; I chose the former, but later discovered that this had been based on a bureaucratic mistake by the military authorities, for the latter would have been far cheaper!

This had been my first venture outside Europe, and the sole occasion upon which I have undertaken a longish sea voyage. It was thus a considerable adventure, which was carried out in entirety at the British Government's expense. Although then twenty-eight years old, I had on two occasions travelled around the European continent, but never before into the torrid zone.

I therefore set out from Tilbury docks on 31st December 1960 on my first venture to the 'tropics'. The 9,000 ton SS *Calabar*[1] (named after the city in eastern Nigeria) built as long ago as 1935 which was to convey me to Nigeria, was owned by the Liverpool-based shipping company, Elder Dempster.

History of sea transport from Britain to West Africa

Prior to 1849 there had not been regular shipping from Liverpool to West Africa. Until then, Liverpool's merchants had had to charter a vessel to provide transport. Ships thus came in all sorts of shapes and sizes. In 1852, the *African Steam Ship Company* was formed. In 1869, the *British and African Steam Navigation Company* was added. Later in the century, these two lines were merged under the auspices of Elder Dempster and Co. Incidentally, this firm was to play a significant rôle in the 'scramble for Africa' beginning in 1884, and was thus to take part in shaping the British Empire. Abolition of the slave-trade had by the mid-*nineteenth* century left the West African economy at a low ebb; however, it began to recover with development of the 'ground-nut' industry.

Meanwhile, palm oil and palm kernels became in great demand due to:

- The industrial revolution
- Soap and candle manufacture
- Margarine production.

In the 1880s cocoa was added (especially from the Gold Coast), and for a limited period cotton, rubber, teak and mahogany were also added to this list. After rail services were started, and the interior became more accessible, gold, tin and coal were transported from the mines, and other minerals followed. By the late *nineteenth* and early *twentieth* centuries, commerce was escalating, standardised currency developed, and direct bargaining became less common.

Sir Alfred Jones (1845-1909) is automatically associated with the Elder-Dempster line; he first went to sea as a cabin boy with the *African Steam Ship Company* at age fourteen years; several years later he became a junior clerk in a firm, Laird and Fletcher. Jones had then become involved with two Scots – Alexander Elder and John Dempster – and was invited to become a junior partner in the Elder Dempster Line Ltd. In 1884 however, he bought them out and soon became the dominant figure in Liverpool's West African sea trade (*see* Chapter 1). Despite his great prosperity, he held native Africans in high esteem and was seriously concerned at the high levels of morbidity and mortality in West Africa which lay behind the term the 'white man's grave'.

Such was the background to the Liverpool shipping industry which was to transport me to Nigeria.[2]

London to Lagos

The voyage from London to Lagos in 1961 was punctuated by three short stops – Madeira, Freetown (Sierra Leone), and Takoradi (Ghana). In former days, the West Coast of Africa was to the marines full of obstacles; the *sand bar* made landfall difficult. In fact, Dakar, Senegal and Freetown, Sierra Leone were the only two locations possessing a natural harbour.

Madeira, the first port of call, a small autonomous Portuguese island, the capital city of which is Funchal, was founded in 1421. The island is 55 km long and 22 km wide, with numerous rugged mountains. Probably known to the Phoenicians, the island was rediscovered by a Portuguese navigator by the name of Joño Gonçalves Zarco. Wine (bearing the name of the island) has been an important export since the *seventeenth* century. Madeira is also reputed to have possessed the first sugar cane plantation in the world.[3]

The next port of call was Freetown (*see* Chapter 1), the capital of Sierra Leone. The earliest inhabitants of Sierra Leone had been the Buloms; the largest of the present ethnic groups (the Mende and Temme) arrived in the *fifteenth* century, when there was a Portuguese fort on the site of what is now Freetown. European ships visited the coastal areas of Sierra Leone for slave-trading and ivory dealing. This country occupies 71,740 sq km and has four distinct physical regions: a coastal swamp, a thickly wooded mountainous region, grassland and wooded country of the interior plains, and an eastern plateau containing several mountains. The economy is based on agriculture (rice, cassava, coffee, cacao and palm oil) and mining (diamonds, iron ore, and bauxite [an aluminium ore]). Wildlife in Sierra Leone includes: chimpanzees, tigers, crocodiles and numerous bird species. Freetown had in fact been founded in 1787 (*see* below) by a group of abolitionists as a centre for freed and runaway slaves. In 1808, the coastal settlement became a British colony, and in 1896 a protectorate. The country was to achieve independence in 1961, and to become a republic ten years later. Various military regimes attempted to attain power in the *twentieth* century, when the United Nations (UN) peacekeeping force attempted to suppress political and economic turmoil with only partial success.[4]

The last brief land-fall before Lagos was in the Republic of Ghana (formerly the Gold Coast) – *see also* Chapter 7. Takoradi (to the west of Accra) is the major port, and the one at which SS *Calabar* briefly anchored. Home to some 75 tribes (the largest being the Akan [which includes the Ashanti] and Mossi), Ghana covers 238,533 sq km. The country is generally flat, being dominated by the Volta River basin, and although the north is characterised by grass plains, the southern coastal regions are heavily forested. The economy is based on agriculture (cacao being the major commodity) and mining of gold and diamonds. Wildlife includes lion, leopard and elephant. The modern state is named after an ancient Ghana empire, which flourished in western Sudan -some 800 km north-west of the modern state – until the *thirteenth* century. Although European (Portuguese) exploration began in the *fifteenth* century, when a slave-trading headquarters was established at Elmina (west of Accra – *see* above), it was not until the mid-*eighteenth* century that the Gold Coast became dominated by numerous forts controlled by Dutch, British and Danish merchants. The country became a British Crown colony in 1874, and protectorates over the Ashanti and northern territories were established in 1901; it became independent (with Kwame Nkrumah as president – *see* Chapter 7) as Ghana, in 1957. Since then, numerous military coups have occurred.[5]

I had, in fact, set out on New Year's Eve. In those days, New Year's Day was not a bank-holiday in England (unlike Scotland); during the festive season only Christmas Day and Boxing Day were! Exactly when the winter solstice holiday proliferated into ten days or a fortnight of holiday is unclear to me. My first letter was written some four or five days out of Tilbury.

Letter 1

Elder-Dempster Lines

SS 'Calabar'

Approx 40 miles from Madeira

Wed. 4/1/61

[A] fairly good journey so far, although [the sea was] rough in [the] Bay of Biscay and off [the] Portuguese coast. This being a smallish vessel, [it] rolls very considerably. [A postcard of the same date also records that the sea was very 'rough during the first two days …'].

Fortunately [I] did not suffer from sea-sickness, although [I] felt slightly short of 100% on [the] second two days. [The] majority of passengers [I continued] have experienced this malady – in fact it was not until yesterday that many appeared in the refectory for the first time! Food is excellent, generally speaking.

Weather [has] now improved ++, and in fact is now pretty warm with [a] pleasant breeze. [I] saw [a] subtropical sky last night – beautifully clear and starry, with moon reflection: calm sea – not a sight to be missed.

Due to arrive at Funchal, Madeira [*see* fig 2.1] at 3.00 pm today. I have arranged already to go on [a] conducted tour of [the] island, and intend sampling [the] local wines.

Passengers [are] a very mixed bunch! The bearded giant with whom I share a cabin (and whom you saw) is a Master Mariner who looks after [the] waterways etc in Lagos. Most [of the passengers] are youngish chaps who are either in [the] Colonial Service or [are] working in banks in Accra or Lagos. [The] ship's Doctor is [a] pleasant old boy – whose knowledge of medicine is clearly somewhat limited and who seems to have much trouble from personal sea-sickness!

*Fig 2.1: View of Funchal, the capital city of Madeira.**

Deck games – quoits, table tennis etc are now arranged and I shall no doubt be competing.

I don't know when you'll get this letter – there's no airport in Madeira apparently, so it may be some time.

[I] look forward to hearing from you when I reach Lagos.

Madeira has just come into sight …

Letter 2

Elder-Dempster Lines

SS 'Calabar'

(off Portuguese Guinea)

9/1/61

[We are] due at [Freetown] Sierra Leone tomorrow a.m. Weather now is absolutely superb – the tropical sun is far more powerful than anything one experiences in England. The sea is as calm as a mill-pond. The day now is spent either playing deck-games (quoits, tennis, ping-pong or cricket) or watching dolphins, porpoise, flying fish or the various sea birds – from the lower deck. I now understand why cruises are popular winter pastimes!

Since I last wrote, we have called at Madeira [*see* fig 2.1] – a beautiful island, governed by Portugal. Bananas, oranges, palms, etc grow quite abundantly; geographically the island is entirely mountainous. Like several of the passengers, I undertook a tour of the capital city – Funchal – where we viewed the important monuments and cathedral, tasted the wine ++, partook of a most splendid meal, travelled from the mountain in man-pulled toboggans, rode in bullock carts, viewed the local products – lace and basket work, and had a thoroughly good day.

Following this, we passed through the Canary Islands – Tenerife, Gran Canaria, Las Palmas etc – which we viewed from the ship's radar screen – and then on towards the tropics.

This climate is quite splendid and the night sky with moon reflecting across the sea is quite unbelievable.

I have practised a minimal amount of medicine on the voyage. It's amazing how popular one becomes and how many hypochondriacs one meets as soon as they know of one's professional status! I was also called in on a second opinion by the ship's doc today.

I am now wearing shorts and open-neck shirts and [am] still perspiring considerably. Also getting rather sunburnt.

I heard the England-SA [South Africa][6] game on [the] radio [and] wonder if Ian [my brother] attended! I am quite out of touch with the news generally – haven't even heard the New Year's honours list[7] as yet. I gather though that England is fairly cold at present.

Several interesting activities take place in the evenings – from 'horse racing' this evening, to films – we have seen in fact 'I'm all right Jack', & K [Kenneth] More in 'Man in the Moon' this week …

My major reading material during that voyage was a novel by A J Cronin – *The Citadel*, which almost certainly had an effect, largely subliminal, on the remainder of my career. It is the story of temptation and financial greed by a member of the medical profession; not that such is by any means confined to medicine, a recent example being that of a former *labour* prime-minister of Britain – Anthony Blair.

In 1924, a recent medical graduate of St Andrew's University – Andrew Manson – largely for altruistic reasons, applied for and was appointed to two successive posts in South Wales. In the first of these at Drineffy, he eventually fell foul of the sister of the ailing head of his general practice and had to resign. In the second, at Aberalaw – a colliery town some thirty miles distant – after marrying a Drineffy school-mistress (Christine) he again won a great deal of respect for his medical practice, but upset an influential segment of the mining population. While there however, he gained both the MRCP (which I had recently obtained) and the MD for his work on occupational pulmonary disease. For the former he was asked questions on *malaria* and 'an obscure West African parasite'! Research for the latter involved guinea-pigs, and this led to protests from a vociferous minority (anti-vivisectionists), and his eventual resignation.

Wide acclaim for his pulmonary researches (*see* above) led to appointment as Medical Officer of a Parliamentary Committee in London. However, this transpired to be largely bureaucratic and Manson desperately missed the *clinical* aspects of medicine. He thus resigned from this also, and set up as a general practitioner in a deprived area of Paddington.

At this point, he became associated with several 'west end' charlatans who put financial gain ahead of patient care. This was most distressing and distasteful to Christine – who eventually died as a result of a road accident. He was also appointed to a venerable hospital – the Victoria Chest Hospital (thus confirming his acceptance by the establishment), where the elderly physicians were very wary of newly introduced techniques and were still prescribing 'cod liver oil and malt' for pulmonary tuberculosis.

A wide-ranging dinner conversation with two old colleagues from South Wales concluded that Andrew had become far too money-oriented and that his morals were rapidly slipping. Eventually he came to his senses when he realised that this money-making set with whom he had become involved knew little about medicine or surgery, and were in fact potentially dangerous. He decided to sell his practice and form a *group* practice at Stanborough with these two former South Wales colleagues. But it was too late; he became seriously depressed and furthermore the Welbeck Street set reported him to the General Medical Council for associating with a non-medical man in treating a former colleague's daughter for advanced tuberculosis – from which she duly recovered. He narrowly avoided the ignominy of being 'struck-off'.

The moral of the novel is that financial greed frequently ends in disaster! In fact this narrative is exemplified in the *fourteenth*-century proverb: 'Pride goes before a fall'.[8]

I met many people on that voyage, but have kept in touch with very few. I did however meet Michael Egan, who I think was due to take on a teaching rôle 'up country' in Nigeria, at Greenwich many years later, when we were able to discuss that interesting fortnight on SS *Calabar*.

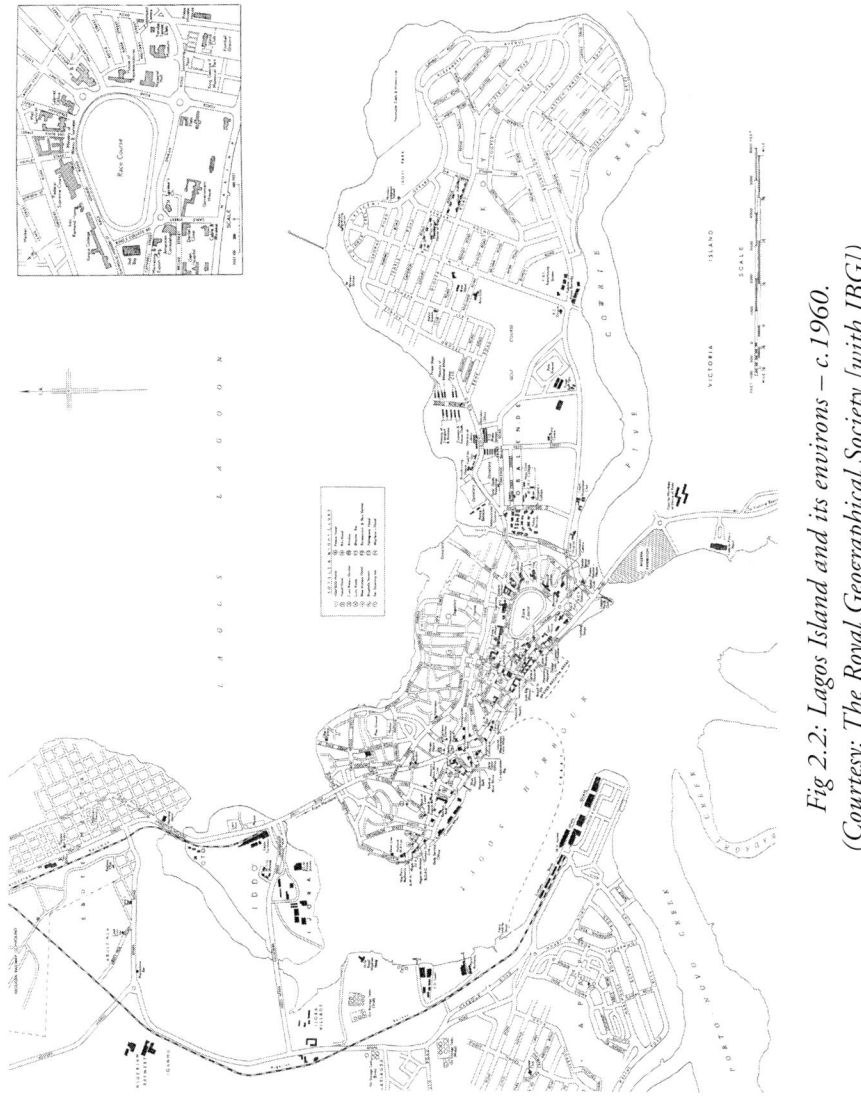

Fig. 2.2: Lagos Island and its environs – c.1960. (Courtesy: The Royal Geographical Society [with IBG]).

So much then for the voyage! The next chapter will describe my introduction to what was to be my 'home' in Nigeria for the forthcoming fifteen months, and more specifically record my initial impressions as viewed from a suburb of Lagos – Yaba (*see* fig 2.2).

References and notes

1. P N Davies. *The Trade Makers: Elder Dempster in West Africa 1852-1972.* London: Allen & Unwin 1973: photograph – plate 30 (p 449).
2. Ibid: 526; P N Davies. *Sir Alfred Jones: Shipping Entrepreneur par Excellence.* London: Europa Publications Ltd 1978; J Walvin. *The Slave Trade.* London: Thames and Hudson Ltd 2011: 47-65. [*See also*: J G Reed. Jones, Sir Alfred Lewis (1845-1909). In: H C G Matthew, B Harrison (eds). *Oxford Dictionary of National Biography.* Oxford: Oxford University Press 2004; 30: 436-8.]
3. Anonymous. Madeira. In: *Britannica Concise Encyclopedia.* London: Encyclopedia In. 2002: 1134.
4. Ibid. Sierra Leone: 1705.
5. Ibid. Ghana: 741.
6. This rugby union match was played at Twickenham on 7th January 1961. The final score was: England 0, South Africa 5.
7. This was written at a time when the 'honour's list' was still far less politicised and farcical than it is today. Professional men (and women) of merit were included, and it was *not* entirely dominated by individuals from the entertainment and sports worlds – most of whose achievements are genetically determined, and many of whom are already in receipt of accolades from their respective professional organisations. (See also: D Epstein. *The Sports Gene.* London: Yellow Jersey Press 2013: 338; E Smith. *Why Gareth's Genes are Worth £85 Million.* 2013; London Times 2 [September 3rd]: 2-3.)
8. A J Cronin. *The Citadel.* London: Vista 1996: 380; E Knowles (ed). *The Oxford Dictionary of Quotations* 6th ed. Oxford: Oxford University Press 2004: 1140.

3

Lagos, Nigeria
January–March 1961

After some seven or eight months of NS I had eventually arrived at my *overseas* posting – Yaba, Nigeria. The voyage had taken about two weeks, significantly faster by far than the first documented expedition to the 'interior' of West Africa in 1832 – which from Liverpool to the Niger Delta took three months! It was therefore now time to adapt to a totally new environment, a new civilization, a climate to which I was unaccustomed, and medicine of an entirely unfamiliar pattern. I had had absolutely no previous experience of any of these!

We safely crossed the infamous 'Lagos Bar' (*see* Chapter 1), which had been a significant hazard to shipping in the *nineteenth* century and took its awful toll of human lives and ships. Indeed at one time (before dredging was begun in 1914) it was virtually impossible to approach Lagos by sea safely, and imported goods, etc., were frequently landed at a port well away from Lagos.

Whilst disembarking from *SS Calabar*, a hot topic of conversation amongst those who knew Lagos and had lived there before, was the recent death (probably caused by malaria) of the bishop's wife, who had apparently been well known to many on board.

My correspondence from Yaba, and indeed from West Africa, to my parents in England began shortly after arrival in mid-January 1961:

Letter 3

Monday 16th Jan 1961

Military Hosp.

Yaba, Lagos

[I] arrived on time at 2:00pm Sat. (14/1/61) at Apapa[1], Lagos – where the C.O. [Commanding Officer][2] his wife and the administrative officer were waiting to welcome me.

I'm now in the process of getting organised in my quarters at the mess [*see* figs 3.1 and 3.2]. They don't have windows – only wire nettings – there is an enormous fan which revolves day & night. Mosquito nets have to be used all the time. [I was to be *without* air-conditioning in an old and dilapidated army hut, probably built during the Second World War (1939-45)] for my fifteen months in Nigeria.] Outside my back door are palms, banana trees etc., etc.

Every 2-3 yards one sees enormous lizards of the most exotic colours running here and there. I've not seen many mosquitoes as yet. [I was however, to take daily proguanil (Paludrine) as a malaria prophylactic throughout my West Coast days (*see* Chapter 1) – with a 100% success rate.]

The only other NS officer resident in the Yaba Officers' mess was David Daniels[3] of the Royal Army Dental Corps (*see* fig 3.3). He had already served in Nigeria for several months.

Weather is pretty warm and very humid – a ¼-mile walk is sufficient to soak one's shirt all the way through [*see* above]. But so far I have not disliked the climate at all – the process of acclimatisation on the ship was no doubt of great benefit.

Yesterday, i.e. approx 21 hours after arrival, I played cricket for the [Nigerian] Army in Lagos. Although I failed [with] the bat, I managed to hold two difficult catches and was therefore quite pleased with the day's play – we won by 20 runs …

Re – papers, we get '*The [Daily] Telegraph*' every day – airmail edition – only 24-48 hrs late. Consequently I don't see any great necessity for further journals – thanks for suggesting this however!…

Called at Freetown & Takoradi, Ghana [*see* Chapters 2 and 7] during [the]

Fig 3.1: The Officers' Mess at Yaba.

Fig 3.2: Living accommodation at Yaba.

Fig 3.3: Captain David Daniels of the Royal Army Dental Corps – a fellow NS conscript (a & b) and mess member.
(a) contemporary photograph, and (b) entry in the Dentist's Register for 1962.

THE DENTISTS REGISTER for 1962

Original Certificate Number.	Name.	Address.	Date of Registration.	Title to Registration and Additional Qualifications.
35307	**Daniels**, David Higham ..	2, *Leeson road, Bournemouth, Hants*......	1959, Mar. 17	L.D.S. R.C.S. Eng., 1959; B.D.S. U. Lond., 1959
29763	**Daniels**, Douglas Percy ..	1, *Clarendon place, Leamington Spa*......	1950, Dec. 30	L.D.S. U. Birm., 1950; L.D.S. R.C.S. Eng., 1951
20987	**Daniels**, John Edmund, v.r.d.	3, *Brandling park, Newcastle-on-Tyne*, 2	1925, July 20	L.D.S. U. Durh., 1925
16358	**Daniels**, John Henry	64, *Durham road, Stockton-on-Tees*	1922, Aug. 21	Dentists Act, 1921
24220	**Daniels**, John O'Connor ..	288, *Park road, London*, n.8	1935, Dec. 13	L.D.S. R.C.S. Eng., 1935
37208	**Daniels**, Stacey Myles ...	193, *Priory road, Hull, Yorks*...........	1961, Sept. 26	B.D.S. U. Sheff., 1961; M.B., Ch.B. 1957, U. Brist.

latter part of [the] voyage – v.interesting [and I] bought one or two small souvenirs. …

I recall, very early in my Yaba residence, young Nigerian men climbing trees outside my back door in order to obtain palm-oil, which was at that time both a very valuable commodity and also an important cooking ingredient which was widely used – as my first scientific publication verified (*see* Chapter 6).

Lagos (*see also Chapter 1*)

In the 1960s, Lagos was the capital city of Nigeria (*see* Prologue). Its origin as a city had had much to do with several early governors, and of course Lord Lugard (*see* Chapter 1) as did modern Nigeria itself.

The small Yoruba kingdom of Lagos had been ceded to Britain by its ruler Dosunmu on 6th August 1861. Britain had by then had a foothold in Lagos, as well as other parts of the West Coast, for some fifteen years; however, this was the first time that she had actually occupied land in what was to become present-day Nigeria. From these small beginnings the country had by 1961 grown into a large international commercial centre, with a population of over 350,000 individuals. In addition, Lagos then possessed a large sea-port as well as an international airport.

The beginning of British influence in Lagos had actually begun as far back as 1849, when the superintendent of the naval establishment, John Beecroft (*see* Chapter 1) – who was based and subsequently died at Fernando Po (an island 32 km away in the Atlantic Ocean), which served the squadron whose task it was to suppress the slave-trade   was appointed that year as Consul for the Bights of Biafra and Benin. This was the first step in British occupation of Lagos. Many freed slaves had returned from Brazil to their place of origin – Lagos, where they had built many of the Brazilian-style (Portuguese) buildings – still to be seen in present-day Nigeria (*see* below).

For a time, beginning in 1868, Lagos Colony came under the administration of the Gold Coast Colony and early information on Lagos can be found in the Gold Coast Government Gazettes. This arrangement terminated in 1886 however, when Lagos became independent. Soon after this, the *National African Company* became the *Royal Niger Company*.

Between 1864 and 72, Lagos rapidly expanded under the then Governor, Sir John Glover (1829-1920). In 1886, it became an independent colony, and various official buildings (*see* below) had been built. There was a tendency for early governors to prioritise what seemed at the time the wrong projects. For example, the railway was given priority over a much needed sanitary system, and as early as 1898, the streets of Lagos were apparently illuminated by electric light, before this was available in most towns and cities of Britain! About this time a new Government House – the 'Iron Coffin' (demolished in 1960) – was built to replace the original structure. The present Government House dates from 1892 and two years later, a public electricity supply was provided. In 1899, Sir William MacGregor (1847-1919) arrived as Governor, and his major interest, as was that of Sir Ronald Ross (1857-1932) – fresh from his discoveries in India – was to improve sanitation and drain the malarious swamps. MacGregor also initiated the regular taking of quinine and proper wells. Two years later, both the Lagos Government Railway linking Lagos to Ibadan, and the Carter Bridge were opened. The Lagos Steam Tramway was also inaugurated. These early years of the *twentieth* century also saw the building of several more public buildings (including the General Hospital). It was not until 1925 however, that building began on Ikoyi Island. The *new* docks at Apapa had been completed the previous year.

Most ordinary houses in Lagos were and are still roofed with corrugated iron, the reason being that formerly thatch was used and there had been in consequence a number of sizeable fires.

By the outbreak of the Second World War in 1939, the Yaba Estate had been completed, and people were encouraged, despite a great deal of local opposition, to emigrate there from Lagos Island, which had by then become grossly overcrowded.

By 1961, public transport in Lagos remained extremely inadequate; there were simply too many cars, and traffic congestion on Carter Bridge proved a very serious obstacle to progress. Lagos in 1961 was in fact a busy and bustling city, which was also grossly overcrowded.[4]

The daytime temperature in Lagos rises to around 110°F (43°C), and humidity is high for most of the year, although towards the end of February, the Harmattan brings drier, cooler (although dust-laden) air from the Sahara; this is usually followed by a somewhat sultry period in the prelude to the rains in April or May.

Following my introduction to Lagos, I was to spend the next few days exploring the city – with which I was to become very familiar during the following fifteen months (*see* fig 3.4):

Fig 3.4: Map showing the position of Lagos, and that part of Nigeria which would become familiar to me during fifteen months in West Africa. (Anonymous. The Collins World Atlas. London: William Collins Sons and Co Ltd. 1979: 70-1.)

Letter 4

Military Hospital

Yaba, Lagos

28th January 1961

… I'm giving [this letter] to one of the chaps who is flying back to London today, so that he may post it in England tomorrow. …

[I'm] still enjoying life here – sailing, swimming, surfing etc, in the lagoon at Lagos. Tennis [in the Mess compound] every evening.

I have purchased a transistor set – which picks up [the] BBC overseas service.

Much of this past week has been spent at a paediatric conference held in Lagos – organised by [the] West Africa Council for Medical Research. [I] met rather surprisingly a Nigerian chap [Dr Ishaya Audu[5]], with whom I was on the house at [the (Royal) Brompton [Hospital]. The reception [at the conference] was given by the Government of Nigeria at the Federal Palace Hotel, Lagos – the best and newest hotel in Nigeria [*see* fig 3.5] . The Governor-General [Dr Nnamdi Azikiwe (1904-96) (*see* fig 3.6)][6] and [Government] ministers were all present.

I was also introduced into RNA routine and the Military Hospital, Yaba – my 'place of work' for the following year and more (*see* figs 3.7-3.9).

As an Army Officer in Lagos one is really quite an important personage. The entire strength of the Nigerian Army [formerly the Royal West African Frontier Force] is only 7,000. I'm now completely fitted out in my uniform – bush jacket, tropical type hat [*see* figs 3.10 and 3.11], etc. [I omitted to mention *mosquito boots* – which were still worn by expatriates after dark – a reminder of past times]. As I haven't yet purchased a car, I use the Army transport for my visits to Lagos – which is [overall] fairly satisfactory.

I was soon to become acquainted with the 'shanty towns' (*see* figs 3.12 and 3.13) , the Marina – laid down by the first governor (*see* figs 3.14 and 3.15), and Carter Bridge – named after a former governor of Lagos, Sir Gilbert Carter (1848-1927) (*see* fig 3.16.). My letter resumed:

> The poverty of these primitive peoples is almost unbelievable – most of the local inhabitants seem to live and sleep in the roads or on the pavements – many of course sleep the best part of the day – the pace of life is such that it is almost brought to a standstill! Beggars – usually lepers, sit on most of the street corners; everyone asks you for cash ['dash'] wherever you go.
>
> [I] saw a Russian ballet show at the Lagos stadium last Monday – very enjoyable, attended by the Governor General [*see* above], etc.
>
> [I] hope to go up country for some 60 miles or so tomorrow – so [I] shall probably get my first glimpse of [the] jungle [*i.e.* rural Nigeria].

I was to become familiar with the Yoruba people (*see* fig 3.17), the Lagoon (*see* figs 3.18-3.20), Victoria Beach (*see* fig 3.21) and also the local architecture[7]

Fig 3.5: Above: The Federal Palace Hotel, Lagos – probably the best hotel in Nigeria at that time*. (See also Chapter 6.)

Fig 3.6: Right: Dr Nnamdi Azikiwe – President of Nigeria in 1961*. (See also Chapter Five.)

Fig 3.7: Above: A Royal Nigerian soldier 'on guard'.
Fig 3.8: Right: The author in the formal uniform of the Royal Nigerian Army.
Fig 3.9: Below: The Military Hospital – Yaba, Lagos.

Fig 3.10: My ward sister, a Sierra Leonian.
Fig 3.11: The author dressed in mess kit.

Fig 3.12: Group of Nigerian children in one of the local 'shanty towns'.

Fig 3.13: Street scene in a Lagos 'shanty town'.

Fig 3.14: A view of the Marina, Lagos, which had been established by an early Governor*. (See also Chapter 5.)

Fig 3.15: Ship docked at the Lagos Marina.

Fig 3.16: Carter Bridge, Lagos (named after a former Governor, Sir Gilbert Carter) – a well known 'bottle-neck' for traffic.

Fig 3.17: Left: Example of a Yoruba woman in local dress.

Fig 3.18: Below: Lagos lagoon, viewed from State House*. (See also Chapter 8.)

Fig 3.19 : Lagos lagoon*.

Fig 3.20: Fishing vessels in the Lagos lagoon.

Fig 3.21: Above: Fishermen on Victoria beach, Lagos*. (See also Chapter 6.)
Fig 3.22: Bottom left: Broad Street, Lagos – viewed from Independence Square*. (See also Chapter 8.)
Fig 3.23: Bottom right: Street scene in urban Lagos.

Fig 3.24: Scene in a Lagos suburb.

Fig 3.25: An example of the Italianate style of building in Lagos.

Fig 3.26: Above: The nineteenth century Anglican cathedral – situated on the Lagos Marina*. (See also Chapter 8.)
Fig 3.27: Left: East End of the Anglican cathedral.

Fig 3.28: Foundation stone laid by Bishop Leslie Gordon Vining, the first Anglican Archbishop of West Africa. (The foundation stone of Bethel Cathedral.)

– both traditional and contemporary (*see* figs 3.22-3.25). The first Governor (in fact, the Acting Consul) had been the merchant, William McCoskry. British security was such that freed slaves from Brazil returned to the land of their birth (Nigeria); with them came their Portuguese building skills (*see* above). A subsequent Governor, Glover (*see* above) between 1864 and '72 both extended the marina, built the present-day Broad Street and other thoroughfares, and established wharves, warehouses and business facilities.

I was also made aware of the extensive Nigerian literature, and introduced to the Lagos Museum (*see* Chapter 6) soon after arrival – the historical treasures (largely from Benin) and the art collection being of particular interest. I have to admit that I viewed the artefacts there primarily from an *enjoyment* angle. Dennis Duerden has, however, in the *Nigeria Magazine*, differentiated ways of viewing Nigerian art into three erudite ways: (1) an historical/archaeological approach, beginning with the discovery of the Benin bronzes in 1938, and seeking *unity* of development, (2) an ethnological slant centred either on smaller or larger ethnic groups, and (3) through the eyes of an artist.[8]

A building of particular interest was the *nineteenth* century [in fact it was not completed until 1928] Anglican cathedral (*see* figs 3.26-3.27).

A familiar sight in Lagos as in all other parts of Nigeria, which I duly recorded, were the numerous 'mammy wagons' which conveyed many, often overweight, women from place to place. I continued:

> [I] certainly haven't received any of the letters you mention – so presumably they have left England by sea. I should think that one of the liners is due in Lagos very shortly. [I] shall be grateful if you will check up and reprimand the appropriate postal authorities! …

I also at that time ventured further afield as letter no. 5 indicates:

Letter 5

Military Hospital

Lagos, Nigeria

6th Feb 1961

… Yes I still like the climate – the only unfortunate factors are:

a) the amount of sleep required, and

b) the fact that thought processes are somewhat retarded by the temperature. It therefore takes rather longer to perform the same amount of work as in more temperate climates.

Re – mail:

1. I have failed to receive your letter addressed to Freetown (Sierra Leone).

2. The '*Practitioner*' arrived today; I've not in fact asked for this to be sent 'direct' since it is only [a] monthly [publication].

3. I would much appreciate it if you would send on *all* mail other than any obviously advertising material – i.e. including Harveian Soc., Osler Club, etc. etc.

4. If the certificate for my MRCP [*see* Prologue] arrives, please keep it in a safe place until my return. Don't bother to open or unroll it!

5. I have still not received the letters you forwarded in early Jan.

Sorry to hear of the death of great aunt Clara [sister of my paternal grandmother][9] – please convey my condolences.

The trip up country last week [with David Daniels] was one of extreme fascination – my first glimpse of the lush, dense tropical vegetation. I also saw cactae [sic] growing in great abundance for the first time at a town called Badagry [*see* Chapter 4]. This latter settlement is of very considerable interest from the slave-trading viewpoint, since [many] of the [West] African slaves left the [west coast] by this route.[10] We saw the chains used for this purpose and also met the two oldest inhabitants who were said to have been associated with the latter part of the 'trading'. This town is also of interest in that the first [Christian] missionaries who entered Nigeria[11] entered at this point – consequently the *southern* half is primarily a Christian community (very largely R.C. [Roman Catholic]) whilst the *northern* territories are Mohammedan – this religion having entered via the travellers crossing the Sahara – the desert trains in fact come down as far as Kano [in the north of Nigeria]. [We] also called at several local markets[12] – one of the most interesting 'stalls' was one devoted to witch-doctoring!

It was in 1562, that Sir John Hawkins (1532-95) initiated English participation in the *Atlantic* slave-trade. Hawkins in fact made three voyages to exploit what was then a fast growing industry – in 1562-3, 1564-5, and 1567-9, the last proving a failure. This trade had of course long been in progress *within* Africa – probably for thousands of years – and it was the Portuguese who were the first Europeans to exploit it (*see* Chapter 1). It was from these small beginnings that the vast trade in slaves to the new world developed. By 1642, Portuguese influence had in effect been eliminated, and the slave-trade was dominated by the French and British; by 1800 the vast majority of slaves were transported across the Atlantic in *British* ships (*see* Chapter 2).

At a more down-to-earth level, African middlemen became intermediaries between the source of supply and expatriates on the coast. Some coastal chiefs such as those in Lagos, Bonny and Dahomey developed their territories as slave-trading kingdoms. Profitability of trading in slaves to African middlemen and European merchants alike became so high that other commercial interests were virtually ignored! Disease (*see* Chapter 1) was such a problem to the expatriate that trade was in fact largely left to native chiefs.

In 1807, slave-trading was declared illegal in Britain and the last slaver (*Kitty's Amelia*) left Liverpool in July of that year. By 1825, Denmark, the USA, Sweden, Netherlands, France and Brazil had followed suit, and several years before that, Portugal and Spain had agreed to limit activity to 'seas south of the equator', thus eliminating West Africa. However, it was not until 1888 that legal slave-owning was abolished by *all* nations, and even after that slave-trading continued illegally!

The history of the entry of the Christian missionaries is interesting. They in effect largely followed in the footsteps of the traders, and by far the first were Portuguese, who carried the Roman Catholic 'message' as early as the late *sixteenth* century. For more than two centuries, Roman Catholic priests had by 1961 been working in those regions. They had been active at Abeokuta – some fifty miles north of Lagos, for many years. Protestant missionaries, however, did not arrive until the mid-*nineteenth* century under the banner of the *Church Missionary Society* (CMS). They were followed by several other protestant groups, who rapidly penetrated many parts of western Nigeria, including Abeokuta (*see* above and below).

Christianity today in western Nigeria thrives; the heart of the church in 1961 was in Bethel Cathedral, Broad St, Lagos (*see* fig 3.28) – when completed, the tallest building in Lagos. Methodists, Baptists and Roman Catholics, as well as Anglicans also produced significant contributions. In 1960, it is said, Nigeria claimed more ordained clergy than any other country in Africa, and furthermore, they were generally better trained! An article by J B Webster in the *Nigeria Magazine* [*see* Ref 11] gives both a history of Christianity in Nigeria, and also the 'state-of-play' in 1961.

While in Badagry, we were told of examples of infanticide – especially involving twin births. Although we had no proof that this was currently in operation, it is well known that it was widely practised in the *nineteenth* century, and probably more recently.[13]

[I] shall be going up to Ibadan[14] tomorrow (approx 90 miles [north-east of Lagos]) to see a patient – the wife of a British officer there.

[I] spent yesterday watching a cricket match on the Lagos racecourse – Africans v Europeans – which the former won easily (their team contained most of the Nigerian test team!).

[I] have now purchased a 35mm camera so am taking colour transparencies wherever I go.

Food in the mess is mainly European – although we get a fair sprinkling of African menus – very interesting. …

Letter 6

Military Hosp.

Lagos, Nigeria

16th February 1961

… I wrote early last week (I think 6/2/61!) so [I] am surprised you had failed to get it when you wrote. Although [the] mail is good on the whole, it is however very unpredictable. [I] have received several letters during [the] past 1/52, (sent on). I have now been here 5/52, nearly – how quickly the time passes! Yes, you can assure Uncle Stephen[15] that … life here is thoroughly enjoyable, most of all the climate.

[I] attended a race meeting on the Lagos race course [*see* fig 3.29] last Sat p.m. – quite an exciting occasion. This sport seems to suit the temperament of these [Nigerian] people. They become extraordinarily excited, and look most attractive & colourful in the vast numbers in which they turn out for such an occasion. The local tribe is that of the Yoruba, who wear a huge variety of blue costumes – blues of all shades and tints.[16] I took a goodly number of photographs – so [I] hope they will capture the scenes.

My first set of films arrived back from processing this a.m.– apart from 2 rather over-exposed pictures, these are highly satisfactory (they have to go to England for processing – the return postage is paid by Kodak!).

I think I was due to go to Ibadan – the new University centre, and largest town in West Africa – the day after that upon which I last wrote. We had an excellent day; [I] swam in a most beautiful swimming bath, looked over the £5,000,000 new University College Hospital [*see* fig 3.30][17] – attached to [the] University of London, whose degrees are taken here – and explored the town generally. The trip is approx 90 miles [145 km] from Lagos & the roads are absolutely awful.

[I] met a police officer last week (Nigerian) who was on the *Calabar* [*see* Chapter 2] – splendid chap who is [a] cousin of the Minister of Transport for [the] federation. He took me around the night clubs and high spots[18] of Lagos last Saturday evening. [It was] most interesting being conducted by a local inhabitant. I found myself the only European in two of the clubs – quite an odd sensation. One is very much the object of attention, and being associated with medicine they have considerable respect for one's status it seems!

Fig 3.29: Scene at a race meeting in Lagos*. (See also Chapter 9.)

Fig 3.30: Aerial view of University College Hospital, Ibadan* – about ninety miles northeast of Lagos. (See also Chapter 5.)

[I] continue to find myself fairly busy – plenty of good medicine [I had charge of a ward of Nigerian non-commissioned soldiers – most suffering from tuberculosis, schistosomiasis, or lobar pneumonia – as well as officers (many of them expatriates) in a separate ward]. [I] met [the] Countess of Limerick[19] (Vice President of [the] Red Cross) last week. She came to hand over to the Nigerian government. Quite a pleasant old girl; [she] looked round my beds in [the] Military hospital.

Letter 7

Lagos, Nigeria

25th February 1961

[I] received the 'Freetown' letter [*see* above] yesterday – posted [on] 4/1/61.

[The] weather is particularly hot at present; for the past 2/52 a wind known as the 'Harmattan'[20] blows down to Nigeria from the Sahara. At this point however, & until the rains commence in April, there is no wind and things become somewhat parched and dusty. Nevertheless, it's very pleasant indeed to be able to lie in the sun at any time of the day and even plan outings some weeks hence knowing what the weather will be like.

More cricket, sailing and swimming during this week. Tomorrow a couple of us are going for a trip across the lagoon with the General [Maj-Gen Norman Foster[21]] the G.O.C. [General Officer Commanding the] Nigerian Army.

There was a certain amount of [unrest] here last week – following Lumumba's[22] death. Owing to a couple of riots in Lagos, we were not allowed from the mess on Friday or Saturday. The U.S. and Belgian embassies were attacked & the windows smashed – in fact a fair amount of damage was done in Lagos – I was interested that this [matter] was not reported in the English newspapers. All is [now] peaceful again however!

[I] spent a most interesting evening yesterday – visited the home of a chap called Ihekama who was on the *Calabar* with me [*see* Chapter 2]. He had collected [his] entire family together to welcome him back from the U.K. so we had a delightful evening of tribal songs & entertainment. He is organising an evening of tribal dancing for us in the near future. The normal run of Europeans here doesn't of course mix with the Africans to any great extent but live[s] an absurdly superficial existence in English clubs & hotels – so this is a somewhat unusual experience out here. You would be amazed at the prestige value of a visit to the U.K. on the part of the Nigerians. In fact they have a pidgin English expression for such a person – 'a been to'!

26/2/61 – 7.30pm

[I] have just returned from my day with the General [*see* above]! Excellent day; lunch at his chalet on a tropical beach [Lighthouse Beach[23]] near Lagos – sat between General and Brigadier [Goulson] – quite distinguished company. Also surfing; a most enjoyable sport.

Post seems to be coming through fairly well [now] – although odd letters take up to ten days by air. There's little rhyme or reason behind it all. …

[It is] very difficult to think of crocuses and daffodils in this climate! The tropical flowers are quite exquisite – especially the 'flame of the forest'.

There are so many social engagements that it's almost impossible to get any reading done at all. It's the practical experience that matters however.

By now I had settled into a fairly routine pattern of daily life, and the relative novelty of a medical officer's daily programme in a tropical country had to some extent, worn off!

Letter 8

Military Hospital,

Lagos, Nigeria

5th March 1961

… Life continues much the same – everything is taken rather good humouredly and light heartedly here; the Nigerian temperament really is rather charming – I suppose due entirely to the climatic factors – so that no-one really worries about anything; one's existence is one of absolute euphoria. Of course this makes working with Nigerians somewhat difficult for, although very well meaning, it is virtually impossible to get anything positive done unless you watch every movement. Nevertheless they are pleasant to work with and extraordinarily good company.

[I] spent Sunday at Victoria beach [another sandy beach, where members of a local religious sect – the Cherubim's & Seraphim's – congregated], Lagos – this is I suppose the 'Brighton' or 'Southend' of Nigeria, the main difference being that the crowds are composed of negroid races [Africans], and produce a rather different colour scheme. In fact, we didn't stay here but walked some 2-3 miles along the tropical, palm lined beach – and passed in so doing several local fishing villages. The native fishing boats – hollowed out of solid trunks, are rather beautifully decorated with carvings and somewhat bizarre painting[s]. They object however to photography [*see* below] – & in fact I understand that Europeans are not infrequently attacked [for taking photographs] in this part of the world!

7/3/61. [I] have just returned from a shopping expedition in Lagos – the stores – Kingsway, UTC, Leventis, etc are almost identical with such … establishment[s] in the UK – with the exception that the most popular section probably is the soft drinks dept! I find that one can pick up a pretty good pair of binoculars for £10 here – so I may well buy a pair in the near future.

Heard from Ian [my brother] 3-4 days ago & also received a very interesting book[24] upon Nigerian history, as a [late 29th] birthday present. … He mentioned his proposed Australia trip – a most excellent idea, I would have thought.

[The] post seems to be fairly satisfactory [now] although somewhat irregular. In the fairly near future, a communication re '*The Medical Directory*' will arrive – this is rather important, so please airmail it (it looks rather like a circular but is of far more importance).

Interested to hear of your Swiss trip – pity you'll miss the winter sports season! Yes, take my camera by all means – there's a film already inside it. Perhaps you'll send me the prints when you develop it. …

Letter 9

Lagos, Nigeria

14th March 1961

[The] surface mail seems rather delayed at present.

There is a suggestion that the rainy season may not be far off here. We've had 2-3 storms during the last week – all at night – and my word, tropical storms so far as I can see make the worst European type [of] storm a mere shower. Nevertheless the daytime weather is unchanged – [I] played cricket on Sunday in very hot weather indeed.

[I] heard a rather impressive display (or recital) of native music on Sat. evening, with native harps, drums etc.

There's considerable interest here, quite naturally, in the Prime Ministers' conference in London [this opened on 8 March at Lancaster House, and South Africa ultimately withdrew from the Commonwealth] – particularly of course on the S.A [South Africa] issue, & especially on the view put forward by the Nigerian P.M. – Alhaji Sir Abubakar Tafawa Balewa[25] – I think that is right!

Next weekend – i.e. Sat. and Monday is a public holiday here to celebrate the Mohammedan festival, Id el Fitr – which marks, of course, the end of Ramadan – during which the devout Muslim eats nothing from dawn till dusk & in fact cannot even swallow his saliva (officially) during this period. Consequently during this period they become so irritable that they are I gather almost unemployable.

[I] hope to get up to Ibadan on Saturday and may stay for the weekend – one of the chaps in the mess [David Daniels – the dentist] is playing hockey against the University so I may accompany him.

Of course in fact Easter is not far off – must be very early this year – what date do you leave for [Switzerland]?

The *Calabar* [*see* Chapter 2] sailed into Lagos again on Sat. – the first time since my arrival – exactly 2/12 previously – how the time flies!

I've had the 'misfortune' to have been elected Messing member for the next 3/12 – so [I] am in fact responsible for arranging menus etc for that period. [I] started with a rather successful Mess dinner last Friday. Since I was also the newest member of the mess, I was also the Vice Chairman, or 'Mr Vice' as Army tradition has it – consequently one's duty is to stay until the last member of the mess has left – on this occasion the Colonel [Commanding Officer] stayed 'knocking back' scotch until 5.00am! There is of course no draught beer here so the staple [brew] is either Star beer – a local product [or] Carlsberg, Heineken or Becks.

Still plenty of medicine to keep me pretty well occupied from 8.00-2.00![26]
…

Letter 10

                                                        Military Hosp.,

                                                        Lagos, Nigeria

                                                        20th March 1961

… I have two suggestions re – [late] birthday present:-

a) 'The Reluctant Surgeon'[27] – Kobler (Heinemann) 21/=.

b) 'Primitive Physic, or an easy & natural method of curing most diseases'.[28] John Wesley. (Epworth Press) 12/6.

I wonder if you would arrange with a reputable bookshop, eg H K Lewis & Co, to send the following book to me:- *Manson's Tropical Diseases* – edited by Sir Philip Manson-Bahr – 15th ed (1960).[29] I don't know the price but I think it's approx 4 guineas. If you pay in the first instance I'll forward a cheque in due course. (It would be better to let the bookshop do the packing I should think). [Interestingly I was to become the editor of this venerable book much later; in fact I edited the 20-22nd editions].

[I] returned yesterday evening from an extremely enjoyable weekend at Ibadan [*see* above] – as I previously wrote, I went primarily to watch hockey. In the event, the team was a player short – consequently I was roped in & therefore played against University College on what is said to be the best hockey pitch in Nigeria. Again [I] looked around the splendid buildings of this vast new Univ. College – and on Sat. evening attended a performance of 'The Gondoliers' at the Arts Theatre. An interesting performance – the cast being mixed – i.e. coloured and white. It was indeed rather strange to walk into a theatre filled with white faces again! I was very pleased to meet several people I previously knew, including two graduates from my year at the Royal Free Hospital – they are doing Path [pathology] jobs at U.C.H. Ibadan – and I have provisionally arranged to visit them and see a few patients etc in due course.

We were admirably entertained by the C.O. [Commanding Officer] at Ibadan – who has recently been a patient of mine in a colonial type house – some 30-40 years old. Called at Abeokuta [a former centre of slave-dealing – *see* figs 3.31-3.33] on the return journey and visited the M.O. [Medical Officer] there – who is a [*Royal*] London H. [Hospital] graduate.

Fig 3.31: View of Abeokuta – some sixty miles north of Lagos.

Fig 3.32: Abeokuta market-place.

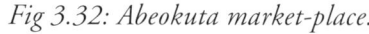

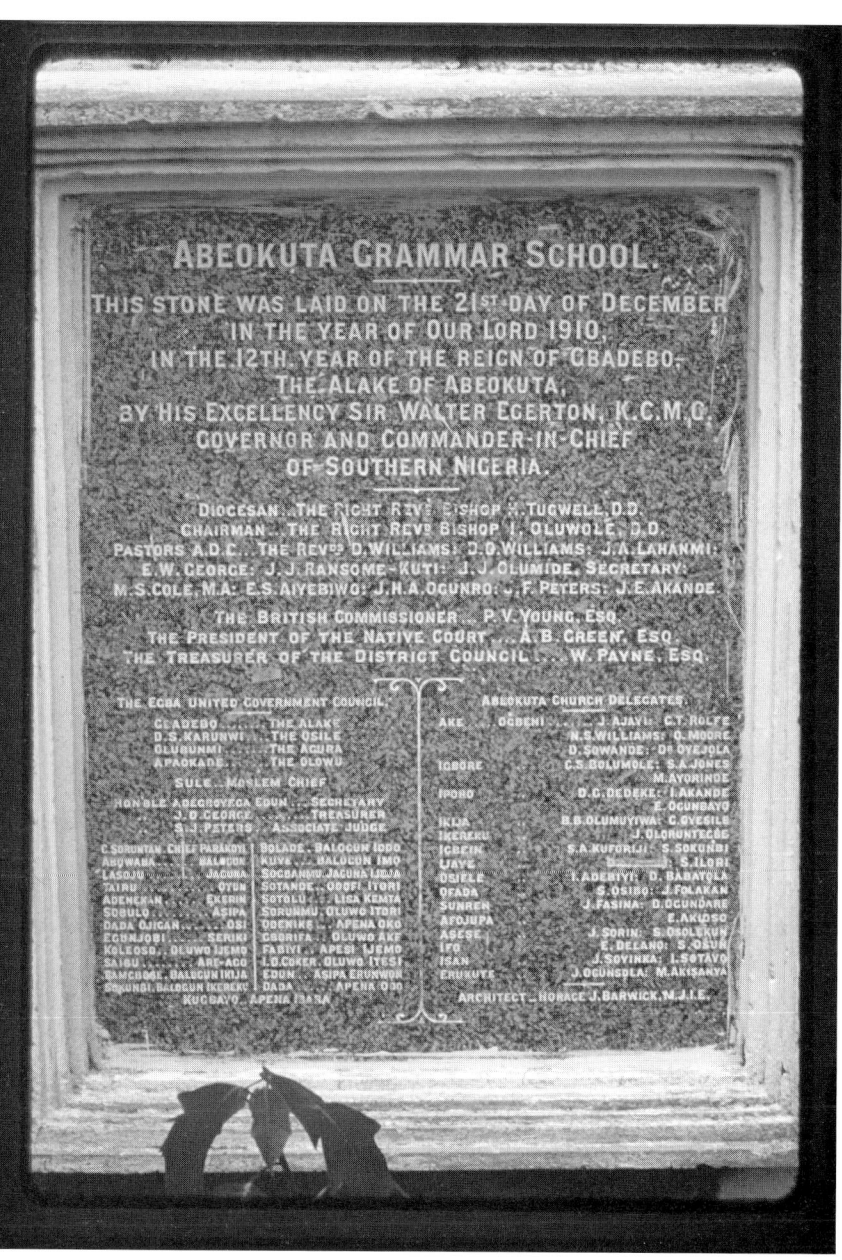

Fig 3.33: Plaque at the grammar school, Abeokuta.

Everyone here is delighted at the withdrawal of S.A. [South Africa] from Commonwealth.[30] I would think that this decision has caused the avoidance of extensive demonstrations in Lagos, amongst other places. …

I gather that your warm spell (record breaking, I believe) has given way to a colder spell. Should be far warmer in Switzerland.

[I] shall probably be purchasing a car during [the] next 2/52 or so – from the General's A.D.C. [Lieutenant Kennedy] who is returning to the U.K. – 18/12 old 'Dauphine' [which has] only done 7,000 miles.

Trust all is well.

Letter 11

Military Hospital,

Lagos, Nigeria

29th March 1961

… Yes indeed, a Happy Easter to you all! I see that British Summertime has commenced – so you're now on a par with us I suppose …

The rains have indeed [begun], bringing with them many temporary defects in communication etc. The electricity supply I gather invariably breaks down under these circumstances which in fact it did last Monday.

Had an excellent day on Sunday at Abeokuta [*see* above] – some 60 miles north of Lagos – [I] played cricket for the General's XI – knocked up 24 [and] we won the game after an exciting struggle.

On Monday afternoon [I] visited a local 'prince' or his equivalent in a native village some 80 miles distant – the Odoma of Ishara[31] – His Royal Highness. He is in fact the Chief Whip of the Opposition party. He entertained well and I took several photographs of him in his ceremonial robes – may be going to lunch with him in the near future!

I shall be on duty for part of Easter unfortunately, but hope to get away for [some] of it at least. It had been my original intention to join up with one of the Majors [Stanley Richardson] in the mess and visit Dahomey [now Benin – *see* Chapter 7] – the old French protectorate some 150 miles distant – but this will no doubt have to wait for a future occasion. Owing to the fact that Nigeria is not a diplomatic relation of France, the acquisition of a visa is not easy anyway. They have several game reserves there however, so a visit should be well worthwhile.

The Prime Minister [Baewa – *see* above] was welcomed back [from the London conference] with great enthusiasm – and things seem politically very settled at present.

I heard today from one of the [Royal Herbert Hospital] Woolwich chaps – he is going shortly to the Cameroons [*now* Cameroon – to the south-east of Nigeria]. Most of my contemporaries have [now] been posted, mainly to rather second rate places so I seem to have been fairly fortunate.

Hope to have my car by Tuesday – so [I] shall at long last be mobile!

I will indeed collect any stamps which come my way. … Some of the local ones are quite picturesque.

So far [the] rain has not excluded the sun by any means – but when in fact the rains are really set I believe there is v. little sun indeed.

Oxford for the boat race! … [32]

With a car I should with luck be able to start a little 'private practice' amongst the European population of Lagos – should broaden the scope somewhat.

Hope your trip goes well – may hear from you in [Switzerland].

So, my first three months in Nigeria were coming to a close. My knowledge of *tropical medicine* still left much to be desired. However, I now had my own transport, and had duly adapted to Yaba and the 'foreign' life-style. However, the novelty of it all was by now beginning to wane as subsequent chapters will demonstrate.

References and notes

1. A K Earl. Nigeria's Ports. *Nigeria Mag* 1962 (March): 27-33.
2. **Lt-Col Denis Hugh Robert Montgomery**, MC, RAMC, had graduated from St Thomas's Hospital (MRCS, LRCP) in 1938. In 1961, he was the Commanding Officer of the Military Hospital, Yaba, Lagos.
3. **David Higham Daniels** BDS (London), Captain, Royal Army Dental Corps was, like me, a conscript undergoing two years of National Service. He had qualified in dentistry a mere two years previously (1959).
4. E Thorp. *Ladder of Bones.* London: Jonathan Cape 1956: 320; N S Miller. The beginnings of modern Lagos: progress over 100 years. *Nigeria Mag* 1961 (August): 106-21; [*See also*: O Nzekwu (ed). Lagos 1861-1961. *Nigeria Mag* 1961 (August): 91-190; A B Laotan. Brazilian influence on Lagos. *Nigeria Mag* 1961 (August): 156-65].
5. **Ishaya Audu** FRCPE, who was originally from northern Nigeria, had graduated from University College Ibadan, and King's College Hospital, London (MB BS [London]) in 1954. He then undertook several junior appointments both in Nigeria and Britain. (*See*: Anonymous. Audu, Ishara Sha'aibu. *Medical Directory 1980*: 92).
6. **Dr Nnamdi Azikiwe** (1904-96) was one of the first leaders of the nationalist movement in West Africa and subsequently the first Governor-General and then first President of Nigeria. (*See:* Preface, and Anonymous. Nnamdi Azikiwe. *Times, Lond* 1996: May 14: 19).
7. D J Vickery. Contemporary Nigerian Architecture. *Nigeria Mag* 1962 (June): 44-52, 61-2; N Onwuka. Modern Architecture in Lagos. *Ibid*: 53-60.
8. D Duerden. Nigeria's Art. In: M Crowder (ed). *Nigeria 1960* Lagos: Federal Government Printer 1960: 24-37; P K Allison. Collecting for Nigeria's Museums. *Nigeria Mag* 1963 (June): 125-30; B Fagg. Mining for History. Op cit. *Nigeria 1960:* 38-45; U Beier. Contemporary Nigerian Art. *Nigeria Mag* 1961 (March): 27-51. [*See also:* C Legum. Great Benin: the elusive city. Op cit. *Nigeria 1960:* 157-66; U Beier. Nigerian literature. *Ibid:* 209-18; R Horton. Three Nigerian Novelists. *Nigeria Mag* 1961 (September): 218-24); P O Nsugbe. Oron *Ekpu* figures. *Ibid* (December) 1961: 357-65; K C Murray. Benin Art. *Ibid* 1961: 370-8; H Sassoon. Birom Blacksmithing. *Nigeria Mag* 1962 (September): 25-31; P Eccles. Nupe bronzes. *Ibid* 1962 (June): 13-25].
9. **Clara Lloyd (née Wall)** (187?-1961) was the third child, and second

daughter of Aaron and Sarah Wall of Herefordshire. The Walls were to have three more daughters. One of Clara's sisters was my paternal grandmother – Frances (Fanny) Cook – *see* Chapter 8. (*See also:* G C Cook. *Torrid Disease: memoirs of a tropical physician in the late twentieth century.* St Albans; Tropzam 2011: 297).

10. H Thomas. *The Slave Trade: the History of the Atlantic Slave Trade 1440-1870.* London: Picador 1997: 925. [*See also*: Anonymous. London celebrates the end of slavery. *Times, Lond* 2000: August 2: 2).
11. J B Webster. The African Churches. *Nigeria Mag* 1963 (December): 254-66; E Igwe. Thomas Birch Freeman: pioneer Methodist mission to Nigeria. *Nigeria Mag* 1963 (June): 78-89;
12. O Nzekwu. Kola nut. *Nigeria Mag* 1961 (December): 298-305; S G Ahmed. Grass weaving. *Ibid* 1962 (September): 10-15; L O Ukeje. Weaving in Akwete. *Ibid:* 32-41; E de Negri. Nigerian jewellery. *Ibid:* 42-54; D W MacRow. Crafts of Bida. *Ibid:* 55-60; P O Nsugbe. Cane and raffia work. *Ibid:* 61-6.
13. Op cit. See notes 4 (Thorp) and 10 above.
14. A Mabogunje. Ibadan – Black metropolis. *Nigeria Mag* 1961 (March): 12-26.
15. My mother's older brother (*See*: G C Cook. *Torrid disease: memoirs of a tropical physician in the late twentieth century.* St Albans: Tropzam: 8, 20).
16. E de Negri. Yoruba Women's Costume. *Nigeria Mag* 1962 (March): 4-12; E de Negri. Yoruba Men's Costume. *Ibid* 1962 (June): 4-12. (*See also:* O Nzekwu. Ibo people's costumes. *Ibid:* 1963 [September]: 164-75).
17. Op cit. See note 14 above.
18. The 'night spots' were an integral part of Nigerian life. 'High life' music was played at considerable amplitude, beer was consumed in large amounts, and 'snacks' included peppered snails.
19. Anonymous. Limerick, Dowager Countess of. *Who Was Who, 1981-1990*: 448.
20. A dust-laden breeze blowing from the Sahara desert; it is cool and brings welcome relief from the hot and humid weather which went before it.
21. **Major-General Norman Foster** was a dedicated British soldier who was born in India and before retirement from the Army in 1965 was one of the last British commanders of the RNA. Educated at Westminster School and the Royal Military Academy, Woolwich, he served for a while in the Royal Horse Artillery. During WWII (1939-45) he served in the western desert. Foster had played both cricket and hockey for the Army. He was a most

humble and friendly man. Anonymous. Major-General Norman (Leslie) Foster, CB, DSO (1909-95). *Times, Lond* 1995: February 6: 21.

22. **Patrice Lumumba** (See: Anonymous. *Britannica Concise Encyclopedia* London : Encyclopedia Britannica, Inc 2002 : 1200; M Evans. MI6 agent 'admitted' plot to kill Congo's first democratic leader. *Times*, Lond 2013; April 2: 4; M Evans, F Elliott, C Bremner. Only MI6 can solve mystery of leader's death, says historian. *Ibid*; April 3: 6; B Macintyre. If MI6 had done this killing they'd never tell: the murder of Patrice Lumumba was too brutal and shambolic to have been organised by the Secret Service 'witch'. *Ibid*; April 5 : 29.)

23. This refers to Lighthouse Beach, where surfing was a popular pastime. It was also the site of General Foster's chalet to which he would 'retreat' from Lagos.

24. H J Pedraza. *Borrioboola-Gha: the story of Lokoja, the first British settlement in Nigeria.* London: Oxford University Press 1960: 118. Lokoja was situated at the junction of the Benue and Niger rivers, and played a key rôle in the early British occupation in Nigeria.

25. **Alhaji Sir Abubaka Tafawa Balewa** (1912-66) was the first prime-minister of the Independent State of Nigeria. He was a Muslim from the north of Nigeria, and was killed in the Biafra conflict in 1966. (*See*: Anonymous. *Who Was Who, 1961-1970*: 1099; F Forsyth. *The Biafra Story: the Making of an African Legend.* London: Severn House Publishers Ltd 1969: 288).

26. 8.00 – 14.00 hrs was the accepted working period from Monday until Saturday. Lunch was followed by a siesta and then evening entertainment.

27. J Kobler. *The Reluctant Surgeon.* London: Heinemann 1960: 359.

28. J Wesley. *Primitive Physic, or an Easy and Natural Method of Curing Most Diseases.* London: Epworth Press 1960: 127.

29. P H Manson-Bahr (ed). *Manson's Tropical Diseases: a manual of the diseases of warm climates*. 15th ed. London: Cassell & Co Ltd 1960: 1177. I was subsequently to become editor of this book for the 20th, 21st and 22nd editions.

30. P Catterall (ed). *The Macmillan Diaries II. Prime Minister and after 1957-1966.* London: Pan Books 2011: 363.

31. The Odoma of Ishara was a local dignitary and a high profile Yoruba chief.

32. I well recall listening in the Yaba Officers' Mess to the 107th Oxford-Cambridge boat race with John Snagge commentating, on my transistor radio. Michael Egan, who had travelled with me on SS *Calabar* was also present. In fact Cambridge University won by 4¼ lengths.

4

Lagos, Nigeria
April–June 1961

By April 1961, I had both fully adapted to a new way of life at Yaba, and just about managed to carry out my medical responsibilities at the Military Hospital, although my knowledge of *tropical medicine* remained rudimentary; I had in fact been 'thrown in at the deep end'!

One was still living in the grand 'colonial' style, life being dominated by evening cocktail parties followed by dinners. This was after all only six months or so after Nigerian independence – in October 1960 – from colonial rule, which had lasted precisely a century!

I soon appreciated also that a constant stream of vendors had to be countenanced at the Yaba Officers' mess. They were selling anything, from carved wooden heads (most made in northern Nigeria or the Congo), to tailored items (often 'made to measure'), to the older forms of West Coast currency – cowrie shells and *manillas*. This form of local currency had slowly given way to the modern coinage system, but manillas (no longer legal currency) were certainly still in ready availability in 1961. With manillas in mind, it is perhaps appropriate to refer in some depth to past currency. In the *nineteenth* century, West Coast currency was based on a cumbersome system of cowrie shells. Thorp (*see* Chapter 3 – ref 4) has given examples:

40 cowries = 1 string
27 strings = 1 shilling

When in 1908-9, the British Government introduced a small nickel coin valued at 1/10 penny, people in most parts of Nigeria slowly welcomed it and the cowrie gradually ceased being a form of legal tender. However, it took many years for disappearance of what had become, after about two centuries, the traditional currency. As expected, the city of Lagos adapted most rapidly to this change, but even in other parts of *Western* Nigeria cowrie shells and manillas were still favoured for direct barter. Transition was especially slow in Old Calabar and Cross River districts. In 1911, a 1902 ordinance was repealed and the manilla was no longer legal tender. However, it was not until 1948-9 that the British Government decided to redeem all manillas at a very favourable rate.

Letter 12

Military Hospital,

Lagos, Nigeria

10th April 1961

… We didn't I fancy have quite as quiet an Easter as you! It really was a most varied occasion; we [various members of the (Yaba) Officers Mess] did not as we had previously hoped, go to Dahomey [*see* Chapter 7] (visas are now pretty difficult to come by) but instead spent two days visiting villages in the western region of Nigeria [*see* figs 4.1-4.7] and meeting the local people[1] – we therefore had lunch in a typical mud-hut on one occasion, and at the opposite extreme with the Odoma of Ishara [*see* Chapter 3] – a local dignitary, who I think I previously mentioned – on a very grand style indeed.

We also visited several local markets and villages in the western region (*see* figs 4.8-4.10).

Most of the people were extremely courteous and pleasant. On one occasion however, we did meet a certain amount of hostility. While I was photographing some of the local populace on Good Friday, one of the older gentry decided he wasn't awfully keen on this (many of the local inhabitants subscribe to Voodoo, and cameras contain Ju-ju[2] in this part of the world) and attacked Richardson, one of the Majors living in the mess, & I in a big way. If indeed we had not had two Nigerian soldiers with us, I feel we might not have escaped with the few bruises that we in fact did! Such events are however, few and far between!

Fig 4.1: Group of Nigerians in a local village in western Nigeria.

Fig 4.2: Street scene in a rural part of the western region.

Fig 4.3: Above left: Group of Nigerians – children and adults in rural Nigeria.

Fig 4.4: Left: Young Nigerian woman in rural Nigeria carrying a large calabash.

Fig 4.5: Above right: Group of village-elders in a western Nigerian village.

Fig 4.6: Right: Well-loaded donkey in rural Nigeria.

Fig 4.7: Left: Albino Nigerian boy accompanying a boy with a bicycle. Albinism was not uncommon in the Yoruba population.

Fig 4.8: Below: Local produce at a rural market.

Fig 4.9: Wood carvings at a rural market.

Fig 4.10: An 'alternative medicine' stall at a local market.

With reference to the villages and the 'native huts' I was not clear at that time whether they still buried their dead relations under the floor of their abode. This had certainly been widely done in the past.

On Easter Sunday evening I was invited to join a most interesting party organised by the General [see Chapter 3] to go out on his launch & take part in a barbecue on one of the tropical beaches [Lighthouse beach] – this was rather delightful.

[I] have played cricket and attended many cocktail parties etc during [the] last 1/12.

Rain is still somewhat intermittent – the 'Rains' as such have not really set in apparently. Between the storms however, the air is beautifully clear and Lagos really appears at its best.

I've now purchased the *Dauphine* I earlier mentioned & am engaged in getting used to it – driving around the quieter streets of the neighbourhood during the afternoons. Driving here is pretty difficult – the standard of driving in Lagos must surely be the worst in the world. This is largely because the police are so corrupt ['dash' was in 1961 required for everything] that licences are only issued if a great enough 'tip' is given. …

Letter 13

[Military Hospital]

Lagos, Nigeria

23rd April 1961

… You obviously enjoyed your Swiss trip enormously. Of the towns you mention, I well remember both Zurich and Geneva – the latter I have of course visited on two occasions and know Lac Leman pretty well – indeed I stayed at Lausanne for 2/52 following Robert[3]'s wedding. I shall be interested to know whether my camera functioned satisfactorily. I by the way had a certain amount of trouble with my Voigtlander [camera] – 2-3 films were rather unsatisfactory so I returned it to the dealer with much gross dissatisfaction so they exchanged it for a Leica.[4] I should think that this should be extremely satisfactory.

Things have been relatively quiet of late – with the 'rains' everything becomes grossly disorganised. Even the electricity supply, & to a lesser extent the water supply, fail at frequent intervals – so that many of the evenings are spent in candle light.

Most evenings were therefore spent in the Yaba mess, where after dinner several of us produced slide-shows (particularly when a new batch of slides had arrived), listened to recent records, or played snooker – I frequently played with Daniels (*see* Chapter 3). I continued:

We had a further public holiday for the Queen's [35th] birthday [on April 26th]. That was I think the 6th public holiday since I arrived here – and a further Moslem festival is not far distant.

Most of the UK newspapers seemed pretty dissatisfied with Lloyd[5]'s budget! It didn't appear too bad to me however. The Nigeria budget seemed particularly unambitious.

The cocktail parties, dinner parties, etc go on unrelentlessly. It's good indeed to get away from the semi-moronic army types for a part of one's time.

Sierra Leone [*see* Chapter 2] seems pretty unsettled in this independence week. Riots [are] going on in Freetown [*see* Chapter 2], we gather. Algeria seems to be heading in a rather ominous direction.[6]

[I] had a particularly good day's surfing yesterday, followed by the usual curry lunch. Curry lunch or 'chop' to the locals is the usual Nigerian meal for Sunday lunch – makes a change from roast beef and Yorkshire pud! Very many thanks for ordering my books. I shall look forward to receiving them. I have recently discovered a pretty good medical library in Lagos – which is well within my distance with a car. …

The *medical library* referred to here was at the *West African Council for Medical Research Laboratories.* This had been set up principally as a centre for virus research, especially *Yellow Fever* – which had formerly been an enormous problem in West Africa, and had incidentally been the site of infection of several research workers. The director in 1961 was Dr W G C Bearcroft.

Letter 14

Military Hospital

Lagos, Nigeria

3rd May 1961

… The rains are now pretty well established – so that things appear somewhat gloomy at present. Failures in the electricity supply are becoming increasingly frequent – which is I gather normal for this time of … year – so that most evenings are spent in candle light!

[I] attended a rather interesting wedding last Saturday. One of the African nursing sisters at [the] Military Hospital married the Governor-General's A.D.C [*see* Chapter 3]. An excellent reception with the Governor General – Dr Azikiwe – present.

[I] played a game of hockey yesterday – practice match only.

[I] had an excellent day last Sunday at Tarkwa beach – across the lagoon – very hot indeed! Between the rain at present, things are very pleasant indeed. The atmosphere is so much clearer than at other times.

A further wedding on Saturday next – one of the subalterns [lieutenants] in the mess is getting married so I am [in] the 'guard of honour' – in service dress, sword, etc!

An American ice-show is at present taking place in Lagos – [I] hope to attend before it closes at [the] end of the week.

[I] can't remember whether I told you about my camera. Had considerable trouble, so [I] complained & swapped it for a 'Leica' – should have no further trouble now I hope.

It's rather interesting to sit here and listen to the BBC cricket commentaries – [I] heard part of the Worcester v Australians[7] game – the season will now be in full swing I suppose. Our season has really terminated until the rains have abated I fancy.

I have now established a fairly good liaison with the General Hospital, Lagos They [Dr Paul Grasso[8] particularly] invite me down to see some of their cases from time to time and to perform [needle] liver biopsies for them, which is of considerable interest. Medicine at the Military Hospital is at present not awfully exciting. The problem is that as the NS doctors return to [the] U.K. we are slowly reducing the number of beds. This leaves more time for reading however. …

Incidentally, Grasso (*see* above) proposed me for Fellowship of the *Royal Society of Tropical Medicine and Hygiene*. I was duly elected, and surprisingly became its President from 1993 until 1995.

Letter 15

[Nigerian coat of arms]

… Thanks for organising the books – I enclose a cheque for £3/10/- to cover *Manson's Tropical Diseases* – owing to the fact that I've recently received my back pay from [the] N.H.S [National Health Service], my UK bank balance is satisfactory.

I posted an 'Independence Number' of *The Nigeria Magazine*[9] yesterday – by surface mail – which you should receive in approx 1/12.

Nothing of outstanding note to report. [We] have had a couple of rainless days with brilliantly hot tropical sun – so I've made the most of these sunbathing on … Victoria beach [*see* figs 4.11 and 4.12]. Car [is] running satisfactorily. Cocktail parties [on] most nights now – tonight with the crew of *H.M.S. Leopard* who are paying an official visit to Lagos. Met the ship's doctor yesterday – short service chap who knows Povey! Pretty cushy number – he's on a year's cruise. Povey[10] by the way is still in Northern Ireland I gathered.

My 'antedate' [my NS commenced in May 1960, so I should not normally have been entitled to a captain's pay until May 1961] has now been agreed – so I shall be paid as a Captain from 31/12/60 which is highly satisfactory.

[I] shall be watching Nigeria v Sheffield Wednesday[11] at the National Stadium on Saturday.

[I] saw an American ice-show last week – in the open on a tropical night. Rather paradoxical situation and something of a feat of technical engineering I fancy.

I can't remember whether or not I mentioned last Saturday's wedding. I attended in K.D.S.D [Khaki Drill Service Dress] outfit with sword etc and took part in the guard of honour – all pretty fantastic, for I'd no idea at all

Fig 4.11: Native canoe with group of fisherman at Victoria Beach, Lagos.

Fig 4.12: Group of Nigerians on Victoria Beach.

concerning sword drill – all went well I think, although [I] have yet to see the photographs!

What about my film which was already inside the camera – is it any good?

Yes indeed, [the] *'Practitioner'* and *'Lancet'* arrive satisfactorily about 4-5/52 late….

Fairly interesting medicine…

Letter 16

Military Hospital,

Lagos, Nigeria

Whit Monday 22/5/61

… I've only just discovered that this is Whit Monday! They don't celebrate Whitsun here – & it was only by switching on my radio that I heard the Glamorgan v Australians[12] match & the athletics meeting from White City. (Glamorgan can hardly be said to be on top in this game!).

In fact this lack of a Whitsun holiday is compensated by a further Islam[ic] festival later in the week – when they sacrifice goats etc – so we are due to get Thursday and Friday of this week off. I hope to go with one of the chaps to a place called Jebba which is on the Niger and also to Ilorin some 300 miles distant.

More cocktail parties etc – [I] have been invited to the U.K. High Commissioner's[13] to cocktails next Tuesday. Should be interesting. You'd be amazed at the amount of jealousy amongst the elderly and rather moronic army types if they are left out of a party – it really is amazing.

The rains continue & the mosquitoes are becoming more plentiful and vicious than of late [*see* Chapter 3] – in fact I'm being bitten pretty frequently as I sit writing this letter.

My first film from the 'Leica' [*see* Chapter 3] has been returned from the developers and is eminently satisfactory – shots of Lagos chiefly.

A feature of tropical life which I have not previously mentioned so far as I remember is that of the vast array of flora and fauna. I mention this because as I write, I have just seen two of the most exquisite…moths. The butterflies are equally beautiful as are the birds. Unfortunately, it is not easy to photograph these, unless of course one has a telephoto lens which of course is pretty expensive.

[I] have seen [several] recent 'flicks' of late – of which *A League of Gentlemen* was I think the most amusing. I recommend this if it comes as far as Eastbourne.

I haven't yet seen any of the wedding photographs [*see* Letter 15]. Actually most people have taken colour transparencies – which of course are extremely difficult and expensive to print. So your chances of seeing any are not very great until I return to the UK.

[I] have received many of the forwarded letters – including '*Med Directory*'. Rainy season lasts until [the] end of August I think. …

Letter 17

Military Hospital,

Lagos

28th May 1961

… Since I last wrote the feast of Id-el-Kabir has taken place, which means that I have had 2 days off (once again!). I utilised them in travelling up to the Northern region with a lecturer from the local technical institute. [We] travelled to Ibadan on the first day – and stayed in air-conditioning at a fairly reasonable hotel. Then on to Oyo, Ogbomosho and Ilorin[14] – where we witnessed thousands of these muslims all in national dress flocking to their ceremonies, prayer meetings etc. Pretty colourful overall. Although I was not sufficiently fortunate to see a sacrificial ceremony – they sacrifice rams [*see* fig 4.13] which they have been 'feeding up' for the last few months – for which they pay up to £10 each which, as you will appreciate, is up to 1-2/12 wages – and then roast them. I saw (& photographed) a 'roasting' ceremony. [I] also visited the Oba's palace and looked around the markets and native shops.

Then on to Jebba[15] (approx 280 miles north-east of Lagos) which is situated on the Niger [*see* fig 4.14] – and what a great river this is! I took a couple of reels of photographs there, so hope that [the] results are satis. [I] saw the monument to Mungo Park [1771-1806] and Richard Lander [1804-34] [*see* fig 4.15] – two of the great [British] explorers who perished at this spot [*see* Chapter 1].

Fig 4.13: Northern Nigerian Muslims with goats about to be 'sacrificed' at the feast of Id-el-Kabir.

Fig 4.14: The River Niger at Jebba.

Fig 4.15: Memorial to Mungo Park and Richard Lander (see text) at Jebba, western Nigeria.
Fig 4.16: Sunrise over the River Niger at Jebba.

A H M Kirk-Greene has written an excellent review of the early Nigerian explorers (including Lander and Park) who include Heinrich Barth [1821-65], a German scientist employed by the British Government. The death of Park at Bussa has also been described in scholarly fashion by K Lupton.[16] My letter continued:

> What is of even greater interest however (to you at least) is that I was up in time to see a sunrise over the [River] Niger [*see* fig 4.16] – at 6-00 am – & what a worthwhile thing this was. You know, I've not often seen sunrises unless I've been on duty and attending patients, but this was as good as any I've seen. The reflection of the colours in the calm waters of the Niger [*see* below] – which must be approx 1 mile in width, was quite a sight – I hope my exposures are O.K.
>
> Following a brief visit to Ibadan and U.C.H, we returned to Lagos on Friday evening – to find that my radio had been stolen – which didn't please me greatly. So I spent most of the night driving various C.I.D. chaps around Lagos interviewing people but without success. Thieving here is of course extremely prevalent & I shall be fortunate if I lose nothing more than this. …

It is not widely appreciated that, historically, creation of present-day Nigeria (*see* Chapter 1) indirectly resulted from events around the Niger River. Previously, there was no distinct country on this site, and the West Coast and 'Bight of Benin' were geographically the focus of activity.

The British expedition of the Niger in 1832 was carried out largely from a *commercial* standpoint, whilst that of 1841 ('the Philanthropic Experiment') was mainly *moralistic*, abolition of the trans-Atlantic slave-trade (*see* Chapters 1 and 3), and civilization of Africa (as recommended by an anti-slavery society recently formed by Sir Thomas Fowell Buxton Bt – 1786-1845) being its major aims. Buxton, who was a major figure in the anti-slavery movement, felt that since the naval patrols had been shown to be largely ineffective, they should be maintained solely to guarantee legitimate trade. He was primarily of the opinion that agricultural development would regenerate Africa, and that by setting up a series of trading posts on or near the Niger River, this would serve as an *alternative* to slaving. He wrote: *The African Slave Trade and its Remedy* (1839) which was highly influential in its time. This second expedition had the blessing of the Prince Consort (Albert) (1819-61) himself. Although a model farm at the confluence of the Niger and Benue rivers resulted, morbidity and mortality from 'the fever' (as in the 1832 expedition) proved disastrous.

In the wake of these expeditions, both of which had eventually ended in disaster, mostly from *malaria*, the following two (dated 1854 and 1857-64) sent out by Macgregor Laird with government support, and led by William Balfour Baikie (1824-64) of the R.N. were virtual triumphs. Baikie was born at Kirknall, Orkney, and was medically qualified; he reduced mortality by instituting quinine prophylactically (which the former expeditions had not done), and also by employing many Africans (with inherent immunity) as his crew. He gave an account of his first expedition in his *Narrative of an Exploring voyage up the Rivers Kwora and Benue* which was published in 1856. The Anglican priest, The Reverend Samuel Crowther (c.1809-1891) – a Yoruba (later to be made Bishop of the Niger Territory) – was also attached to this expedition. The sum total of this activity was establishment of the first European settlement at Lokoja at what was to eventually become the future nidus of Nigeria.

However, Britain's major interests on the West Coast were still centred on Lagos and Freetown, and Lokoja's continued existence was thus always on a knife-edge. The slave-trade meanwhile continued unabated; the dream that Lokoja would be an oasis for civilisation and an example to the heathen vanished despite Crowther's efforts, but its commercial rôle continued. Baikie meanwhile died while on his way home in November 1864.

It was at this point that the empire-builder (Sir) George Goldie (1846-1925) entered the scenario, and it was from him that the idea of Nigeria as a single entity largely evolved. The *United* (from 1882, *National*) *Africa Company* emerged in 1879, and soon bought out two large French concerns which had emerged on the Niger scene. The *Royal Niger Company*, at the close of the *nineteenth* century, was able to hand over a vast new territory – which it had administered governmentally and developed commercially – to the British Government, which appreciated that it must assume direct responsibility of this newly created colony – which had come into effect despite threats from both French and Fulani powers.

At this point Brigadier-General (later Lord) Lugard (1858-1945), at the British Government's direction, founded the (*Royal*) *West African Frontier Force*, and the Union flag was raised; Lugard became High Commissioner for *Northern* Nigeria. What Goldie had founded therefore, Lugard – a great soldier-administrator – was to secure and extend. Jebba (*not* Lokoja) became the centre of government, which much later transferred to Kaduna in 1917.[17]

Letter 18

Military Hospital,

Lagos, Nigeria

14th June 1961

… The books have arrived! Yesterday – & in excellent condition to my surprise; even the corners are not 'dog-eared' (I think that's correct). So I've now plenty of reading to do. Very many thanks. …

[I] spent [a] very enjoyable weekend at Ibadan. Examined 82 recruits on Sat. a.m.– and turned down 50-odd![18] Then [I] visited a girl [by the name of] Jeanne Reeve[19] – with whom I studied medicine at [the] Royal Free – who showed me around U.C.H. Ibadan at great length. I saw many patients of considerable interest – for this hospital drains most of Nigeria as far as cases of interest are concerned. It is my intention to go there as often as is possible – to clinical demonstrations, lectures, etc, i.e. if Army allow free transport etc.

Fishing is my main pastime at present – & in fact I have met with a certain degree of success – 3-1½lb [red] schnappers – which I must say made pretty good eating. This sport certainly gets a strong hold of one!

Heard from [Sir] Kenneth Robson[20] today – my old Brompton chief – he is now the Registrar of the Royal College of Physicians of London. Also heard from Dr Foster Carter[21] – my chief at Frimley. Interesting to know what's going on at these respective places.

[I] was very interested in [the] test match[22], particularly [the] last day. The commentary came thro' loud and clear.

Extraordinary to think that midsummer is almost with you in U.K. – how quickly the time goes out here. I've now completed ⅓ (i.e.5/12) of the tour. …

[The] weather here is very variable – two or three days of storms, rain ++, then perhaps a day of hot tropical sun. The storms do an enormous amount of damage to the native houses etc. …

Letter 19

Military Hospital,

Lagos, Nigeria

26th June 1961

… Life here continues in much the same way. Rain ++, although we've had the occasional good day & in fact traversed the lagoon yesterday a.m. to Tarkwa Bay and had a really tropical morning. In fact having had so little sun recently, I feel just slightly sunburned today. Fishing continues but with less success of late. This I gather is usual at this time of the year however.

[I've] had a most hectic week previous to this – dinner parties, etc ++ so [I] shall look forward to a slightly more lethargic & somniferous few days from now onwards. Amazing how so many parties etc keep cropping up!

Ibadan, by the way, is approx 90 miles distant, i.e. 1½ hrs run, but the roads are so bad that one tends to go far less often than one would like. I must however establish more contacts with the university.

[I] received [a] letter from a chap called John Bradley[23] who was at [the Royal Herbert Hospital] Woolwich with me. He has just gone down to the Cameroons [*see* above] – they docked in Lagos harbour *en route* but were not allowed to disembark, which was indeed most unfortunate. It will be interesting to see what happens in Cameroon later in the year. …

Hope you enjoyed your visit to Irthlingborough.[24]

I am by the way collecting most stamps that come within my grasp – so will forward them in due course.

[I] haven't yet heard today's test match[25] commentary, but England have I suppose probably lost by now. [I] must purchase a new transistor one of these days. (Yes indeed, I have just heard of the loss of the match!)

It is my intention to visit further parts of this country – following my Jebba visit, but this will I suppose be unavoidably delayed until the rains are over. My chances of having a look at the Congo[26] don't seem at present too good. A couple of Nigerian doctors have just joined the R.N.A. – so presumably they will be sent down there. No startling news I fancy. …

References and Notes

1. M Langton. The River Ogun: an historical journey. *Nigeria Mag* 1962 (March): 34-44; O Nsekwu. Masquerade. In: M Crowder (ed). *Nigeria 1960:* 188-98.
2. As well as extensive corruption, the power of supernatural agents was very widespread in the Nigerian mind. Hence, the influence of the *ju-ju* on most activities was profound.
3. **Paul Robert** MD was a Swiss medical graduate who had to obtain a British medical qualification to enable him to work as a missionary in South Africa. He was thus a fellow student, who had qualified in 1957, from the Royal Free Hospital School of Medicine. (*See*: Royal Free Hospital School of Medicine. University of London. Directory of Former Students 1995: 57.)
4. A German optical maker, the products of which probably constituted the 'Rolls Royce' of cameras in the 1960s. I paid £100 then, and the camera still provides excellent service.
5. **Selwyn Lloyd** (1904-78) was British Chancellor of the Exchequer in Harold MacMillan's administration from 1961-2. He produced two budgets – the first in April 1961. He was hastily removed from the cabinet on 13th July 1962 on the 'Night of the Long Knives'; many senior observers felt that he had been 'harshly treated'. (*See*: D R Thorpe. Lloyd [John] Selwyn Brooke, Baron Selwyn-Lloyd [1904-1978]. In: H C G Matthew, B Harrison [eds]. *Oxford Dictionary of National Biography.* Oxford: Oxford University Press 2004; 34: 157-63.) [*See also*; P Catterall. *The Macmillan Diaries II. Prime Minister and after 1957-1966.* London: Pan Books 2011: 361, 373-4.] Op cit. Ibid (Catterall): 378, 393, 429.
6. G C Cook. *Torrid Disease: memoirs of a tropical physician in the late twentieth century.* St Albans: Tropzam 2011:66.
7. In those far off days, there was only one international touring team in the entire English cricket season, and 1961 was an 'Australian year'. It was traditional for the tourists to begin with a match against Worcestershire; this game was played on April 29th and May 1st & 2nd. The Australians were dismissed for 177 and 141 respectively, and had it not rained for most of the third day, Worcestershire might well have won. The match was eventually drawn.
8. **Paul Grasso** qualified MD (Malta) in 1949. [*See*: *Medical Directory* 1960: 874]. Grasso incidentally proposed me for membership of the *Royal Society of Tropical Medicine and Hygiene* of which I became president in 1993-5.

9. M Crowder (ed). *Nigeria: a special independence issue of Nigeria Magazine October 1960*. Lagos: Federal Government Printer 1960: 223.
10. **John Sullivan Povey** qualified (MRCS, LRCP) from The Royal Free Hospital School of Medicine in 1957. (*See* Povey, John Sullivan. *Medical Directory 1960:* 1853.) He was well known to me.
11. This soccer match between Nigeria and Sheffield Wednesday was the first encounter between the two, although soccer in Nigeria dates back to the late *nineteenth* century, having been introduced by Scottish Missionaries. During WWII (1939-45), armed forces personnel stimulated a great deal of interest in the game, and by 1961 Nigeria was a nation to be reckoned with in African football!
12. This cricket match was played on May 20th, 22nd and 23rd and was dominated by centuries by the Australians R N Harvey and N C O'Neill. In order to win, the Australians required 117 in just over an hour, and finished on 90 for no wicket. The match was thus drawn.
13. The British High Commissioner (the first for the Federation of Nigeria) was **Viscount Head** PC, MC. He had been a professional soldier, who entered Parliament as the Conservative MP for the Carshalton division of Surrey immediately after WWII (1939-45) in which he rose to the rank of Brigadier. He was soon promoted by Churchill to the position of Secretary of State for War. Head strongly opposed opposition attempts to reduce the period of NS. In October 1956 he was promoted by Eden to the post of Minister of Defence and was thus involved in the Suez crisis. Following three years in Nigeria, he became High Commissioner to the new Federation of Malaysia. Head had been educated at Eton and the Royal Military College, Sandhurst. (*See*: Anonymous. Right Hon Viscount Head: former Conservative Minister of Defence. Anonymous. Right Hon Viscount Head: former Conservative Minister of Defence. *Times, Lond*; 1983: March 30; J Colville. Head, Antony Henry, first Viscount Head [1906-1983]. In: H C G Matthew, B Harrison [eds]. *Oxford Dictionary of National Biography*. Oxford: Oxford University Press 2004; 26: 115-6.)
14. P C Lloyd. Sallah at Ilorin. *Nigeria Mag* 1961 (September): 266-78.
15. Jebba is a small town in western Nigeria – some 50 miles north of Ilorin – situated on the Niger River. (*See*: S de Gramont. *The Strong Brown God: the story of the Niger River*. London: Hart Davis, MacGibbon Ltd 1975: 350.)
16. Both Mungo Park and Richard Lander were West African travellers and explorers; both determined to discover the source and course of the

Niger River. (*See*: K Lupton. The death of Mungo Park at Bussa. *Nigeria Mag* 1962 [March]: 58-70; C Fyfe. Park, Mungo [1771-1806]. In: H C G Matthew, B Harrison [eds]. *Oxford Dictionary of National Biography.* Oxford: Oxford University Press 2004; 42: 637-40; E Baigent. Lander, Richard Lemon [1804-1934]. In: H C G Matthew, B Harrison [eds]. *Oxford Dictionary of National Biography.* Oxford: Oxford University Press 2004; 32: 388-90; C Howard (ed). *West African explorers.* London: Oxford University Press 1951: 598; A H M Kirk-Greene. Nigerian Explorers. In: M Crowder [ed]. *Nigeria: a special independence issue of Nigeria Magazine October 1960*: Lagos: Federal Government Printer 1960: 70-8.) [*See also*: S Kemper. *A Labyrinth of Kingdoms: 10,000 miles through Islamic Africa.* London: W W Norton & Company 2012: 415. (This is an excellent account of explorations – largely in West Africa (Mali and Timbukto included) – by Barth, a relatively unknown German adventurer. His 5 ½ year journey began in 1849; rather than pursuing political matters, he was particularly interested in local cultures, peoples, languages and ancient manuscripts, which remain among the world's greatest treasures.)]

17. H J Petraza. *Borrioboola-Gha*: *the story of Lokoja, the first British settlement in Nigeria.* London: Oxford University Press 1960: 118; Op cit. See note 16 (Kirk-Green) above; A D Galloway. Missionary impact on Nigeria. *Ibid*: 62-9; K O Dike. Trade and the opening up of Nigeria. *Ibid*: 53-61; Anonymous. The rise and fall of the Igala State. *Nigeria Mag* 1964 (March): 17-29; Op cit. See note 15 (S de Gramont) above.

18. A Metteden. Recruiting in the North. *Nigeria Mag* 1962 (March): 13-17. This article contains a photograph of the author (p.15) examining a recruit to the RNA.

19. **Jeanne Reeve** qualified from the Royal Free Hospital School of Medicine (MB, BS) in 1957, and obtained the MC Path In 1964. (*See*: Reeve, Jeanne Daphne. *Medical Directory 1970:* 2172.)

20. **Sir Kenneth Robson** CBE (1909-78) obtained his medical education at Christ's College, Cambridge and the Middlesex Hospital. He was a Consultant Physician at St George's and the (Royal) Brompton Hospitals. From 1961 until 1975 he was 39th Registrar of the Royal College of Physicians. (*See*: [RRB] Robson, Sir Kenneth. *Munk's Roll* 7: 503-5.)

21. **Aylmer Foster-Carter** MD was Physician Superintendent of the (Royal) Brompton Hospital Sanatorium at Frimley, Surrey. He had graduated from Oxford and the Middlesex Hospital. (*See*: Anonymous. Foster-Carter, Aylmer Francis. *Medical Directory 1970:* 857.)

22. The first test match of 1961, against Australia, was played from June 8th-13th at Edgbaston, Birmingham. England won the toss. Without P B H May, England (captained by M C Cowdrey) had a first innings deficit of 321 runs. There were centuries from R Subba Row and E R Dexter (England's second innings) and R N Harvey (Australia). However, the match was plagued by bad light and rain, and ended in a draw.
23. **John Bradley** was in the same NS intake as me at Crookham, and was then posted, like me, to the Royal Herbert Hospital, Woolwich.
24. Irthlingborough, Northamptonshire is a small town where the Cook family (myself included) spent most of World War II (1939-45). (*See*: G C Cook. *Torrid Disease: memoirs of a tropical physician in the late twentieth century.* St Albans: Tropzam 2011: 24-31.)
25. The second test match was played at Lord's on June 22nd-26th 1961 and resulted in England's first defeat since that at Melbourne in 1959, the game having taken three and a half days to complete. M C Cowdrey retained the captaincy and won the toss, making a total of 12 successive coin-wins by England! W M Lawry, the Australian opening batsman scored a century.
26. An outbreak of epidemic viral hepatitis (HAV) was causing disastrous consequences to the United Nations troops in the Congo (now the Congo Democratic Republic). I had volunteered to move there, but in this I failed to escape my duties at Yaba. The Congo had been ruled by Belgium from 1908 until 1960. It replaced the previously privately-owned *Congo Free State* following international outrage over abuses carried out there. The paternalistic and dictatorial Belgian regime came to an abrupt end when the Congo became an independent republic on 30th June 1960. (*See*: Op cit. See note 5 (Catterall): 408, 410-4, 424, 433-7; A Hochschild. *King Leopold's Ghost: a story of greed, terror, and heroism in colonial Africa.* London: MacMillan 1998: 366.)

5

LAGOS, NIGERIA
JULY–SEPTEMBER 1961

This chapter covers the third quarter of 1961. As it illustrates, I was now beginning to focus on 'life after NS'. The remainder of my 'tour' was something to be endured, for the novelty was fast receding! I was, in fact, beginning to look forward to civilian life again, and was counting the weeks until 'demob'.

Letter 20

Military Hospital

Lagos, Nigeria

4th July 1961

… There's not a lot I fancy to report at present. The rain continues++ – we had up to 4" within an hour on Friday. The effect of this upon the roads is of course disastrous – there are now pot-holes up to 12"-18" in even the main roads!

The pathologist here – a chap called Shaw[1] (who was incidentally at [Gonville and] Caius) – has recently returned to [the] U.K. – so from now on I'll be running the pathology [department] as well as the medicine – good experience but pretty hectic in this environment and climate.

I've been listening to [the tennis tournament at] Wimbledon with considerable interest. Yesterday (quarter finals) must have been pretty interesting. I've managed to get two games of hockey every wk for the last two or three weeks – which provides a little much needed exercise. Fishing has slackened off in the last 2/52 – the weather makes the water too muddy at present.

This is however good weather for reading [I recall reading *Ladder of Bones* and other books (*see* Chapter 1 – ref 3)] and I usually manage an hour or so in the afternoon in an air conditioned room [*i.e.* the dentist's clinic].

5/7/61. Today really beats the lot – everywhere is between 6" and 12" deep in water – roads, paths included. If it continues much longer, our rooms (gidas) will be submerged.

[We] won the hockey [match] yesterday evening – fitness improving; scored goal! Heard Truman[2]'s win [in the Ladies semi-finals at Wimbledon] yesterday afternoon. [I] hope to hear [the] semi-finals of [the] men's singles this afternoon – everything [depends] on Sangster…[3]

What is the name of your Lagos neighbours? I've been recently treating a woman called Mrs Ross – who is passing her holiday at Friston – wife of a Police Officer, I fancy. The G.O.C Royal Nigerian Army – Maj.Gen. Foster [*see* Chapter 3] – has recently been my patient. Interesting meeting such people from the doctor-patient angle.

[I] have now purchased a further transistor – Japanese this time, which seems to work better than the previous stolen [one]. Only a matter of time I suppose before this is stolen too.

Mail seems to have come thro' despite the BOAC[4] strike at London airport – exactly how many planes were held up I don't know. [The] Kuwait situation [Iraq forces were building up on the Kuwaiti border] doesn't sound too good at present.[5] …

The 'rains' had really set in by now, and it was clear from my correspondence that it aborted most outdoor activities. However as I was later to point out, it was not as heavy as in other locations where my Woolwich colleagues had landed up!

Letter 21

>Military Hospital
>
>Lagos, Nigeria
>
>14th July 1961

… The rain continues on and off; electricity cuts are so common that approx 50% of [the] evenings are spent in candle-light; the roads are becoming unpassable; and in fact the whole country is, as I was previously warned, 'going bush' (which being interpreted indicates a state of gross inefficiency). Communications are also suffering; telephones are usually out of order, [and] the post is delayed etc etc – so I shall indeed be pleased when the next 2-3/52 have passed. Everything is so damp that mildew and mould form at an alarming pace. Ties are apt, for example, to be covered in a thick film of fungus within 48 hrs, and of course books don't fare too well. Nevertheless this is only a short season and one which is far less annoying than in many other parts of the world, judging from correspondence I have received from Singapore, Malaya and Cameroons – in the latter place where the rainfall is up to 300", it is I gather impossible to put your shoes down for the night without a thick film of myceliae being formed within 24 hrs. The indigenous inhabitants however enjoy the short respite from the tropical heat even though many of them die from exposure, pneumonia, amoebiasis.†[6] I have come to the conclusion that the average Nigerian doesn't like the sun at all!

I listened to much of the tennis from Wimbledon and of course the 3rd test match[7] – quite an afternoon of excitement, last Saturday.

Kuwait seems to be dying down and I must say one hears very little from the Congo at present. With the recruitment of more Nigerian doctors into the Army, I fear my chances of getting a look at the Congo are rapidly diminishing. I hope to get to Ghana [*see* Chapters 2 and 7] later in the year, however. …

---

† *Here, I was referring primarily to amoebic colitis. However, shigellosis and other acute gastrointestinal diseases were also commonplace, so defective were the sanitary systems (see Chapter 3).

Letter 22

Military Hospital

Lagos

22nd July 1961

[The] weather has been better during [the] last 2 days – and in fact I have spent a most enjoyable morning surfing & swimming. Tennis and fishing have been resumed. [I] have seen two films during [the] past week which I recommend – Curt Jurgens in 'The Devil's General' and also 'Saturday Night and Sunday Morning' (X).

… I am hoping to fly up to Kaduna [the *northern* capital city] during the next few weeks, for a few days. Since the Medical Specialist at Kaduna has gone on leave, I am the sole [medical] specialist for Nigeria – and consequently cover the whole of the Royal Nigerian Army, Royal Nigerian Navy, and Police Force (not as arduous as it sounds however!).

The Proms[8] have started & are I gather broadcast fairly regularly on 'BBC Overseas'. There is of course a singular lack of cultural activities here (at least as we know them!).

There is much in the local newspapers about the Governor General's visit to UK etc. You may have seen him on TV I suppose. I consider that the publicity given to Gagarin[9] was quite absurd.

A postcard dated 29th July 1961, depicts a palm-oil collector who has ascended a palm tree, and one dated 1st August (showing the Lagos Marina) refers to the third test-match, and also the fact that it 'Looks as though we (*i.e.* Britain) will] join the common market'.[10]

Letter 23

Military Hospital

Lagos

5th August 1961

[The] weather has become much warmer again in [the] last 10 days, thus making letter writing a task of considerable magnitude. …

I hope by the time this reaches you that the birthday present has arrived – an example of Nigerian workmanship made by the Hausa traders, most of whom live in the *northern* parts of Nigeria, although those particular examples were produced in Lagos.

Leathercraft is widely practised throughout the Northern Province but has achieved international fame only in Sokoto, Kano and Bornu. The following are used: goatskin, sheepskin, and hides from cows, reptiles (crocodile and lizard) and wild animals (leopard and panther). Long ago products from the 'interior' of Africa had been exchanged for salt, dates, and European goods which arrived via the north of the continent. Today products include cushions, briefcases, bags, toys, etc., as well as shoes and saddlery.[11] I continued:

> Since I last wrote I received quite a 'knock' playing hockey and had as a result 5 sutures inserted into my forehead [by Charles Lambert] – the lesion has however united well. Fortunately my right eye was not involved however!
>
> [I] am hoping for a flight to Kaduna in [the] northern region in [the] next week or two (on duty).
>
> We don't get Aug. Bank holiday recognised as you do but have a public holiday later in the month – a Muslim festival I believe. Hope to get away during that weekend.
>
> [I am] listening to the Proms – most Mondays, Wednesdays and Saturdays – fairly good reception.
>
> [I] will write again in [the] near future and send more postcards if you wish. …

It seems that the 'West Coast lethargy' [*see* Letter 24] and boredom had by then overtaken me; I was after all midway through my tour of West Africa.

Two postcards, dated 12th August, show a northern Nigerian camel and rider, and a carving in the Lagos museum, respectively. Taking the dates of the fourth test-match into consideration, I have doubts about the accuracy of the date on the next letter!

Letter 24

Military Hospital

Lagos

18th August 1961

… I seem to be lapsing into the well known West Coast lethargy. They say that writing letters is the most difficult facet of life in the 'white man's grave' (the term [which was] applied until 20-30 yrs ago to this part of Africa as you will I'm sure be aware [*see* Chapter 1], yellow fever, malaria, etc being the main scourges).

Enclosed is a rather amateurish photograph [*see* fig 5.1] taken … of one of my nursing orderlies and myself in the hospital grounds [*see* Chapter 3]. This is working kit; the correct dress is bush jacket etc!

There is a tendency I must say to boredom at present here. I've now completed 7/12 and have exactly 7/12 to do before my homeward trip is due to commence. The continuous succession of dinner part[ies], cocktail part[ies] etc, intermingled with the routine mess life & to a large extent routine run of military hosp. practice, tend to become just a little tedious. In fact there are moments when I look forward slightly impatiently I must admit, to resuming a little 'high powered' London medicine. The time is fast approaching when I shall require to keep my eyes glued to the journals for suitable appointments in civilian life. I'm seriously thinking of joining the T.A. [Territorial Army] following N.S. I am by the way a short service regular at present (not N.S) – this was published in the *London Gazette*[12] a few weeks back. This is to comply with the system whereby I serve in a Commonwealth army.

Weather [is] 'hotting up' – although the evenings and nights are still pretty chilly. I gather [it is] rather like a desert type climate. The months immediately before Christmas – Nov. & Dec. are reputed to be the hottest of the year in Lagos.

[I] have just returned to [the] mess [after] playing in the inter unit hockey final. We lost unfortunately but I gather are due to be presented with 'runners up' medals! …

Yes, [the] post is arriving well at present. An R.C.P. [*Royal College of Physicians*] communication arrived today within 36 hrs from [the] time of posting in Eastbourne. [The] last '*Practitioner*' arrived in approx 3 days

Fig 5.1: The author (right) with one of his nursing orderlies at the Military Hospital, Yaba.

(accidently airmailed I take it). I have mailed two further copies of *Nigeria Magazine*[13] during last week.

Pleased to hear that old Davies posted the parcel satisfactorily. He is a physics lecturer at Lagos technical college and [on] home [leave] in U.K. for 3/12. As far as I remember the handbag [*see* Letter 23] is made of snakeskin. It might be crocodile – I can't just remember which one I finally chose.

Yes indeed I well remember Hailsham [a west-Sussex town] market. Quite a classical Sussex market town as far as I remember.

Test match is heading towards [an] Australian victory.[14] Rather a disgusting exhibition by England during [the] last 2 days. …

Postcards dated 23rd and 27th August show a Nigerian market scene and a carving in the Lagos museum, respectively. There is also reference to the test-match.

Cards dated 1st September show local fishing folk, and a palm-oil collector, respectively.

Letter 25

Military Hospital, Lagos

4th September 1961

… Well, things continue ticking over as usual. I have been [advised] several times by the [military] authorities that I shall be going to Kaduna in the near future, but being regular army chaps, their word counts for very little!

Had a very good day at Badagry [*see* Chapter 3 and figs 5.2-5.5] yesterday. Hope to go to U.C.H. Ibadan for a meeting tomorrow and [I] have arranged a trip to Abeokuta – with guide – next Sunday.

Still practising golf swings at irregular intervals in the mess grounds – but [I] haven't got as far as a course as yet!

[I] have now collected quite a few Nig. stamps which [I] will send in [the] near future – who are they for? [We are] getting quite an influx of Nigerian doctors into the Nig. Army – although of course their standards of medicine leave much to be desired! There's really so much bribery & corruption in this country that they seem almost incapable of managing their own affairs successfully without expatriate intervention.

The Governor General ('Zik') is back, so we had a day of local rejoicing last week – with all of the ships in the harbour dressed overall – quite a fine sight I must say.

[I] am still increasing my collection of photographs and have bought [a] flash-gun, close up attachment etc. (I only hope I do not have to pay too much duty at [London] customs!) …

Cards dated 6th, 11th and 12th September show a 'northern fisherman', a Muslim counting his prayer-beads, and a photograph of the Governor-General, respectively.

Fig 5.2 (a and b): Badagri: a favourite venue for a day's outing, usually on a Sunday.

Fig 5.3: Badagri: chains used in the latter years of the 'slave trade' (see Chapter 1).

Fig 5.4: Badagri: photograph of Bishop Crowder, the first Nigerian to be created an Anglican bishop.

Fig 5.5: David Daniels with Jane Garner – a frequent 'fellow' traveller to Badagri. Her father was an army captain, based at Lagos.

Letter 26

Military Hospital

Lagos

17th September 1961

[I] still haven't managed my trip to the North. Life has been fairly routine recently – the usual run of dinner parties etc. Today has been pretty warm I must say. Spent the morning swimming and afternoon (latter part) playing tennis. I gather from the 'News' that the anti-nuclear demonstration eventually took place this afternoon, despite imprisonments. [The] Ghana situation[15] doesn't sound too good [President Nkrumah eventually took over as Commander of Ghana's armed forces, and dismissed the British Chief of Defence staff]; from information received here it is surprising that the Queen's visit hasn't yet been cancelled. Nkrumah is taking things a little too far.

[I] am still pursuing golf practice but have not as yet played on a course.

I note that British Summertime continues until late Oct. Here of course – 3° from the equator, the days are of identical length throughout the year – it gets light at 7.00am and dark at 7.00pm – this becomes a trifle monotonous after a time.

… The surgeon[16] at [the] Military Hosp. [Lambert] leaves in 1/52 time – so we shall be without surgical coverage! There is a Nat. Service chap with [an] FRCS[17] [Venables] coming out on 17/10/61 I gather, however.

[I] have established some good contacts with [the] BOAC [British Overseas Airways Corporation] people recently; also [the] U.K. High Commission. As soon as you get to know people here, they're on their way home again however!

No [more] news I fear. …

Cards dated 21st and 25th September, show an aerial view of UCH, Ibadan, and the Nigerian House of Representatives.

Letter 27

Military Hospital

Lagos

28th September 1961

… Little news of note. [We have a] public holiday & Independence anniversary celebrations – next Monday. [I] have taken part in numerous parties in [the] last 10 days – for the Surgeon from [the] Military Hosp [*see* above] who has now returned to U.K. Fishing with no success. Golf practice +.

[The] situation in Ghana [is] going from bad to worse;[18] Nkrumah seems to be panicking somewhat. Surely the Queen's visit must be cancelled!

[I] have made provisional bookings for [my] homeward journey – Cairo – Beirut – Jerusalem – Athens – Rome – London. Beginning 6/12 today and taking approx 1/12 – [I] hope this might materialise.

Still no Kaduna trip I fear. Off to Abeokuta for [the] day on Sunday. To Ibadan [*see* fig 5.6] and U.C.H. for a clinical meeting on Tuesday…

Your summer sounds to have been pretty good on the whole. It's already difficult to imagine that it has finished already.

Fig 5.6: A Royal Nigerian Army land-rover, with an army driver; the usual form of my transport to Ibadan.

2nd Oct 1961

Sorry about [the] delay. Independence celebrations you know! Yesterday [I] travelled to Abeokuta and was shown around many of the places and buildings of interest.

This morning, [I] watched the Independence parade etc on the Lagos racecourse. Quite a colourful proceeding with Zik & [the] Prime Minister present. [I] managed to get mixed up in the Prime Minister's procession on [the] way back to the [Yaba] mess; so [I] drove along the crowd-lined roads in [a] land rover following [the] federal ministers etc!

A pretty good first year of independence. ...

A postcard dated 30th September shows the National Hall, Lagos.

References and notes

1. **Alec Shaw** received his medical education at Caius College, Cambridge (William Harvey's [1578-1657] college) and King's College Hospital, London. He graduated B Chir. in 1956 and MB Cambridge the following year. (*See*: Anonymous. Shaw, Alexander John. *Medical Directory 1960*: 2083.)
2. **Christine Truman** [1941-present] won the Ladies' semi-final at Wimbledon, but lost the final to Angela Mortimer 6-4, 4-6, 5-7.
3. **Mike Sangster** (1940-85) failed to reach the final, which was won by R Laver, who beat C R McKinley 6-3, 6-1, 6-4.
4. British Overseas Airways Corporation.
5. P Catterall (ed). *The Macmillan Diaries II: Prime Minister and after 1957-1966.* London: Pan Books 2011: 397-8, 408, 416.
6. G C Cook. Colorectum. In: G C Cook, A I Zumla (eds). *Manson's Tropical Diseases* 22nd ed. Sanders/Elsevier 2003: 125-8.
7. The third test-match against Australia, which was won comfortably by England – with two days to spare – was played at Leeds from 6th-8th July. According to *Wisden*, this is remembered as '[Fred] Trueman's match'; he took 5 wickets for 58 runs in the first innings, and 6 for 30 in the second. P B H May had again taken over the captaincy from M C Cowdrey (who scored 93 in England's first innings) and proceeded to lose the toss!
8. The BBC Promenade concerts; the 67th series opened on 22nd July.
9. **Yuri Gagarin** (1934-68) was a Soviet cosmonaut who in April 1961 had been the first human to travel into space. He never entered space again, and was killed when his jet aircraft crashed during a training flight. (*See*: Gagarin, Yuri (Alekseyevich). *Concise Encyclopedia Britannica* 2002: 711; M Binyon. London finds space to remember first astronaut. *Times, Lond* 2011; July 15: 17.)
10. Op cit. See note 5 above: 372, 383, 386, 392.
11. M S M Kangiwa, A A K Metteden. Leatherwork in Northern Nigeria. *Nigeria Mag* 1962 (September): 3-9.
12. *The London Gazette* (suppl 465038) – 4th July 1961.
13. March 1961 (no 68): 1-90; August 1961 (no 69): 91-194 of *Nigeria Magazine*, which was published quarterly. The March issue contained articles on Ibadan, Nigerian art and Zaria, and the August issue was dedicated to Lagos in its centenary year. My accompanying letter was dated 12th August.

14. The fourth test match of 1961 was played at Old Trafford from 27th July until 1st August. Australia won by 54 runs, and thus retained the Ashes. As *Wisden* reported 'dropped catches (by England) had an important bearing on the result'. Nevertheless, this was keenly fought and was probably the best of the series so far. P B H May scored 95 and K F Barrington 78 in England's first innings. Cowdrey had a throat infection and was thus absent. Interest in the series thus plummeted and the subsequent fifth test (at Kennington Oval on August 17th-22nd), which was drawn seems *not* to have received a mention in my correspondence.
15. Op cit. See note 5 above: 393, 423-5, 436.
16. **Charles Lambert** MRCS qualified at Liverpool University (MRCS, LRCP) in 1952. He was a regular army officer with the rank of Lt-Col. (*See*: Anonymous. Lambert, Charles Graham. *Medical Directory 1970*: 1149.)
17. **Chris Venables** FRCS qualified at the Westminster Hospital (MB, BS) in 1958. He was like me, a National Serviceman. He was later to write several papers and books. (*See*: Anonymous. Venables, Christopher Wilfred. *Medical Directory 1970*: 2661.)
18. Rioting was reported on the streets of Ghana.

6

Lagos, Nigeria
October–December 1961

This chapter contains my correspondence during the last quarter of 1961. As Chapter 7 relates, the run-up to the end of that year was punctuated by a fortnight's tour of four other West African states. Without this break I suspect that I would have been looking forward even more to the end of my Nigerian sojourn.

Postcards, dated 7th and 11th October 1961, show a 'cotton picker', and the Federal Palace Hotel, Lagos, respectively.

Letter 28

Military Hospital

Lagos

16th October 1961

… Still pretty busy; [and we] have had a certain amount of trouble with [the] Commanding Officer (the drunkard) recently [*see* above], and [I] have just completed quite an exciting morning getting him 'ticked off' by the ADMS[1] – i.e. his direct superior.

[I] had dinner with [the] Larges[2] last Wednesday – excellent evening. They seem good types – 'Jimmy & Heather'; quite prosperous you know. Pleasant home, large American car with air conditioning etc – big business types! They invited me out in their motor boat yesterday but owing to [an] ill patient [I] was unable to go. If you see him (he is due to leave here this evening I think, for [the] U.K.) I wonder if you would give him my apologies since

[the] telephones were out of order all day yesterday in Yaba. I have failed again to contact them this a.m.

… Your summer time will be coming to an end by now.

[I] shall fly to Cairo, by Comet I hope & to all of the other places 'en route'. [I] must make the most of the journey back! …

A card dated 17th October, shows Odunlami Street in east Lagos. There is mention of a meeting at which a microbiologist, Prof L P Garrod (1895-1979) from St Bartholomew's Hospital, London, who was in Lagos on a lecture tour, gave a talk.

Letter 29

Military Hospital

Lagos

22/10/61

Well, my trip to Kaduna [*see* figs 6.1-6.3] materialised at long last. I flew up to Kaduna on Wednesday last – at 45 mins notice – to see a Colonel who was rather ill. Excellent journey in a small twin engine [plane] – a Piper 'Aztec' – the only passenger in [a] 5 seater job. [We] flew at 4,000 ft most of the way so [I] had a good view of the Nigerian ecology etc. [One of my lasting recollections was of seeing soccer pitches in many of the remotest villages].

My stay in Kaduna was [all] too short & extremely crowded. I was very impressed with the North [*see* figs 6.4 and 6.5] – the climate [there] is far better – dryer and hotter – than [in] the south. Things are cleaner and there were less 'shanty' towns. [I] also managed to get up to Zaria[3] – one of the few remaining walled cities in Nigeria – and met the Emir (i.e.King of a very large area of N. Nigeria) [*see* figs 6.6-6.8].

Met Audu [*see* Chapter 3] – the chap with whom I was at [the (Royal)] Brompton [Hospital] – who now lives in Kaduna[4] – [I] had dinner with he and his wife on Friday.

I also recall a dinner party with Colonel Neild who was later to become Master of the Worshipful Society of Apothecaries of London, of which I am a Liveryman.

Fig 6.1: Upper-class Moslem resident of Kaduna.

Fig 6.2: Right: Rural scene near Kaduna; this illustrates the usual method of transporting a load in Nigeria.

Fig 6.3: Below: Herd of cattle – near Kaduna.

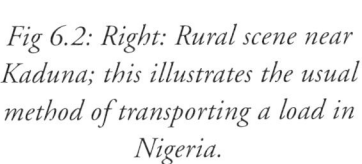

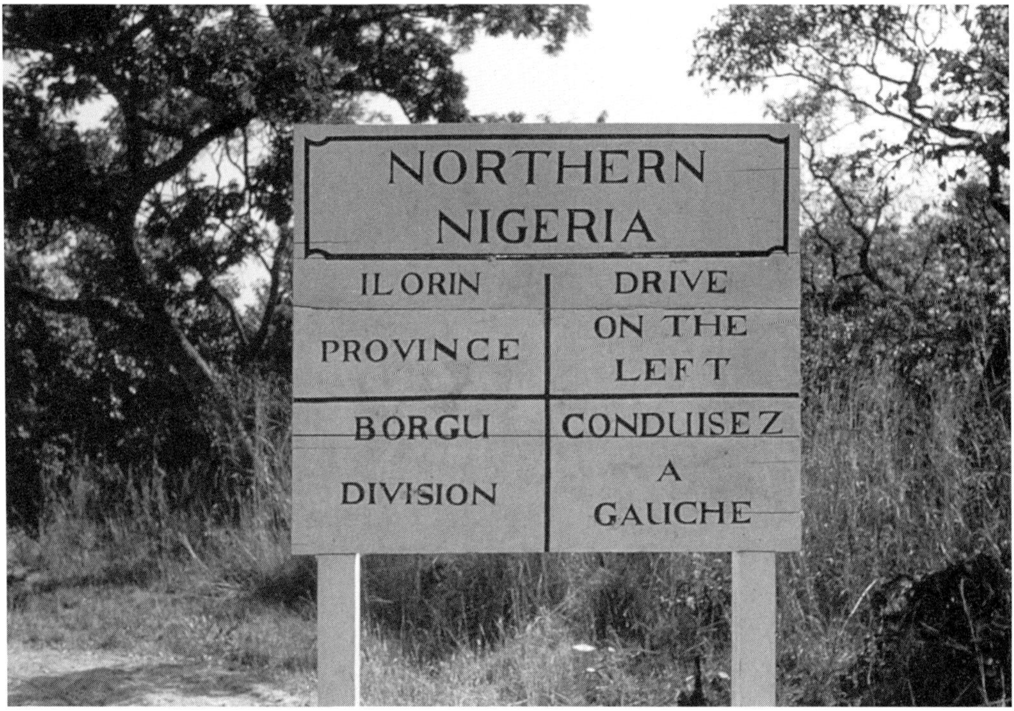
NORTHERN
NIGERIA
ILORIN
PROVINCE
DRIVE
ON THE
LEFT
BORGU
DIVISION
CONDUISEZ
A
GAUCHE

16

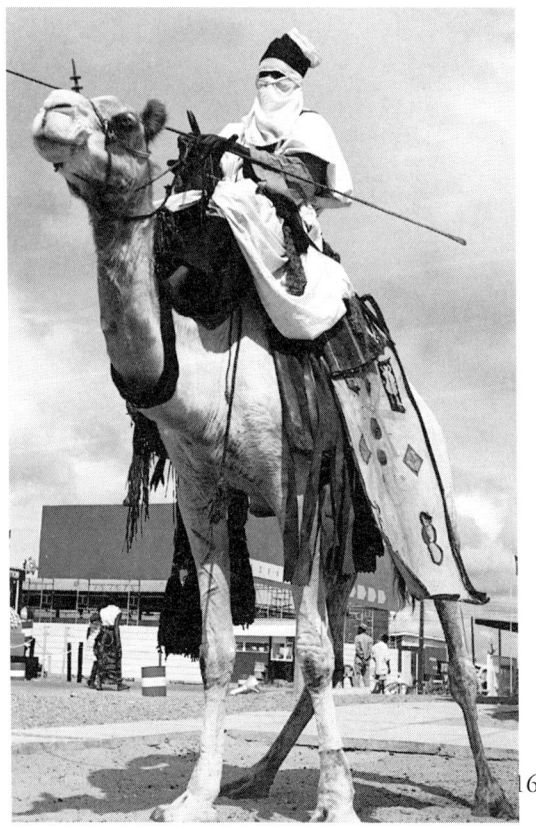

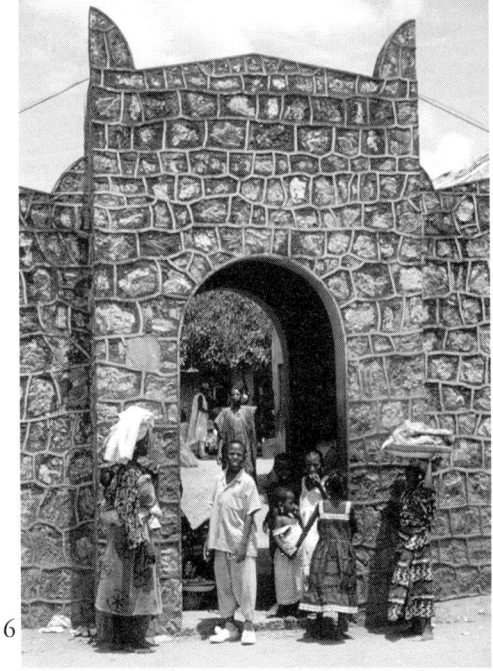

Fig 6.4: Above left: Road sign near Kaduna.

Fig 6.5: Bottom left: Northern camel-rider in ceremonial dress*. (See also Chapter 7.)

Fig 6.6: Bottom right: Zaria: one of the few remaining walled cities in Nigeria.

Fig 6.7: Top right: Zaria: the Emir's palace.

Fig 6.8: Bottom far right: Emir of Zaria in ceremonial dress.

[I] saw the Trypanosomiasis research unit and met the Director[5] (with whom I travelled to Lagos yesterday).

Journey back in a DC3 – again a pleasant journey [although rather bumpy] – excellent view of the towns, rivers, etc – [we] covered the 600-odd miles in approx 2½ hrs, having broken the trip at Ibadan. [I] took some 150 photographs – [I was] v. impressed with my first glimpse of flying. [I] hope to get up to Kaduna again at a later date. …

I had thus been most impressed with *northern* Nigeria. Not only was the climate far better than that of Lagos, but the entire culture (Islamic) seemed more gentle and to my liking. The standards of education seemed better; the whole system was much more to the liking of an Englishman and teaching had after all been founded on British lines, even though most individuals subscribed to Islam. Overall the Moslem Emirates had been allowed to survive the introduction of British rule at the beginning of the twentieth century. The local scenery was also certainly far more to my liking.[6]

Letter 30

Lagos

1/11/61

The news that [National Service – NS] is to be extended by 6/12 has annoyed us all [*i.e.*the conscripts in the RNA] very considerably. I am at present trying to shake off the effects of a very heavy cold which I've had for approx 10 days – so these two facts combined [paint] a pretty black & depressing picture! …

2/11/61. [I] didn't get far yesterday afternoon. [I] have read yesterday's U.K. papers this morning concerning N.S. – there seems little doubt that I'll be affected. [My] cold [is] much improved, however.

[I] have arranged 2/52 local leave – commencing on 4/12 so [I] hope to travel to Dahomey & ? Ghana with the Dentist [David Daniels] here [*see* Chapter 7]. Yes, indeed things are warming up quite considerably.

[I] have done a good deal of sailing [*see* fig 6.9] of late – from Apapa to Tarkwa – approx 6-7 miles – which makes a pretty good change I must say.

[The] films of the North have not yet arrived – [they] should do in [the] next few days!

Fig 6.9: Sailing on the Lagos lagoon.

[The] mail continues to get through pretty well.

My Commanding Officer [*see* Letter 28] has been told not to come back for a second tour (i.e.sacked) so [he] will be replaced by a Nigerian; this is really all rather amusing – since he [Colonel Peters] has only been [in the] R.N.A. for 3/12!

I have applied for a posting to Kaduna, with which I was very impressed. This could well materialise I think. [The] decision to extend N.S. is quite unjust I feel – in fact a disgraceful move by the British Government. …

Cards, dated 7th and 9th November, show an aerial view of the Marina, Lagos; and a local market scene with a number of calabashes in the foreground, respectively.

Letter 31

Military Hospital

Lagos

12th November 1961

[There is] still no definite news of the extension of [the] call-up scheme. The G.O.C. of R.N.A. [*see* Chapter 3] has written directly to the War Office – primarily on my behalf, to get more information on the subject.

A certain amount of mild excitement this week ([or] last week rather). Plans were put into force for the Queen to stay in Lagos should trouble arise in Ghana – so the Army here were all prepared for guards of honour etc, and State House was ready for the royal party. However, such an emergency has not materialised & the Ghana visit seems to be proceeding very successfully.

[The] weather is getting warmer & warmer – the shops are filling up with Christmas cards, paper chains, artificial Christmas trees, decorations etc – and how incongruous the whole situation seems. [I] listened to the commentary upon the Whitehall ceremony [Armistice Day service] this a.m. – how ridiculous to think of the ministers etc standing there in thick coats!

My trip home is nearly finalised I think – [it] should finish with Easter Sunday in Rome & back to U.K. on Easter Monday or Tuesday.

[I] am planning [a] trip to N. Dahomey [*see* Chapter 7] commencing [on] 4/12/61 – with the dentist [David Daniels] from [the] Military Hosp. – for approx 2/52. Hope to see some big game!

The C.O. at [the] Military Hosp. has been told that he will not be returning for a second tour [*see* above] – which I think does not displease anyone in the vicinity. [He] hits the bottle too much!

[The] films from the North have been returned – fairly successful on the whole. The Nig. fellow I met at Kaduna was Dr Ishaya Audu – with whom I worked at [the (Royal)] Brompton [Hospital]. He is now personal physician to the premier of the North & the Sadauna of Sokoto[7] (an important Nigerian dignitary).

[I] have established a fairly good liaison with a pathologist at Birmingham[8] who was a predecessor of mine at [the] M. H. [Military Hospital] Lagos – so [I] am sending various path. specs. by airmail! …

Postcards dated 14th and 16th November depict the Prime-Minister's office, Lagos, and a group of fishermen at the Benue river. I also mention a forthcoming trip to Oyo (in the *western* region).

Letter 32

Lagos

20th November 1961

… No news of great interest I fancy.

More fishing – but without success.

[I] played [in] a cricket [match] yesterday – the first of the season. Made 14 and bowled throughout the innings with moderate success; a dire shortage of bowling talent you will appreciate.

How quickly the time does go! 1/12 until Christmas, and it's getting hotter and hotter as the days pass by. [I] must attempt to purchase some cards I suppose.

No news at all concerning the [proposed] additional 6/12 N.S.

My Commanding Officer [Col. Montgomery] flew back to U.K. on Sat. evening – owing to [an] operation upon his wife. I think in consequence that my chances of a move to Kaduna are thus considerably lessened.

The 'order of the day' was to indigenise (Nigerianise) posts as rapidly as possible, an 'ambition' I have since encountered in other countries of newly 'independent Africa'. I well recall the lightning promotion of a Nigerian to the rank of Brigadier; Ironsi was his name! There is no way in which this rapid promotion would have been possible, or acceptable, in the Royal West African Frontier Force, but anything and everything was conceivable immediately following 'independence'. I continued:

> In the very near future I'll have to commence looking for a suitable [civilian] appointment. It is thus regrettable that the 6/12 extension is so far from being cut and dried.
>
> Plenty of medicine at present. [I] am still corresponding with [the] chap at Birmingham [*see* Letter 31] who is performing various investigations for me. We've got one paper[9] almost ready for submission to the journals I

think. [I] have now performed 130 liver biopsies[10] which must be as many as anyone has done in West Africa I should think!

Little news I fear …

A card, dated 29th November, shows a Lagos hair-plaiter at work. I mention on the card that I shall shortly be leaving on my West African tour (*see* Chapter 7).

Letter 33

Military Hospital

Lagos

1st December 1961

[We are] setting off tomorrow for the Grand Tour – due back in Lagos on 16/12 – just in time for Christmas.

I was very interested to hear that James [my paternal uncle][11] is receiving [an] Hon. Doctorate from Nsukka University. We shall probably go through the town towards the end of the trip [which in the event we did not] – it's approx 50 miles N. of Enugu,[12] the capital of the *Eastern* region.

Encouraging news about [the proposed extension of] N.S. The G.O.C. (Maj-General Foster) has received a reply to his enquiry – from the War Office. It seems that the services of N.S. R.A.M.C. officers in seconded countries are most unlikely to be required for [a] further 6/12. B.A.O.R.[13] is being retained *en masse* with as little alteration as possible, so that most of the chaps serving in Germany will be affected…

Your weather sounds pretty awful. The last few days here have been very hot indeed. Work continues as usual. I'm communicating fairly frequently with [the] pathologist at Birmingham [*see* above] – and am sending a considerable amount of material – chiefly liver biopsies, serum [samples] etc. …

[I] will send the odd card during [the] tour. … [*see* Chapter 7].

Although my correspondence so far seems *not* to have described the Lagos museum in detail (*see* Chapter 3) (*see* figs 6.10-6.12), I had throughout my stay in Yaba spent a great deal of time on visits there. Of particular interest of course, were the Benin bronzes, which I had already referred to.

Fig 6.10: Emblem at the entrance to the Lagos museum.

Fig 6.11: Example of Nigerian craftsmanship at the Lagos museum.* (See also Chapter 3.)

Fig 6.12: A Benin bronze artefact at the Lagos museum.

A postcard, dated 27th December (i.e. *after* the tour of West Africa [*see* Chapter 8]), shows a group of fishermen with their 'dug-out' canoes.

The following letter was written *after* the fortnight tour (*see* Chapter 7) of West Africa:

Letter 34

Lagos, 19/12/61

[I] have now settled down again to the Military Hospital routine. And I must say that working under a Nigerian C.O. [Peters] is far better than it was with the drunkard R.A.M.C. Lt. Col. at the helm!

I had intended giving you a ring on Christmas day, but find that every minute of the festive period is & has been booked for some time. I had no idea that a) this was such a popular pastime &/or that b) the Cable &

Telegraph facilities are so inadequate. There's only 3/12 to go now anyway!

[I] am going to dinner with Larges tonight. [I also] received [a] calendar of [the] 'Tiger' from John & Peggy Barratt.[14]

I heard James's conferment of [an] honorary D.Sc. at Nsukka on the Nigerian radio. Unfortunately, the television range is not great enough to reach Lagos from there. I heard nothing of James in Lagos, but gather that he must have changed planes at Lagos airport – due to [the] fact that I received a card yesterday written by Aunt Elsie [his wife] postmarked 'Lagos'! It is I suppose conceivable that he phoned either while we were away or that I was out. Anyway, the ceremony sounded quite impressive – most of the Nigerian political leaders also received honorary degrees. …

References and notes

1. **Howard Iles** was a Colonel in the RAMC, and Assistant Director of Medical Services (ADMS) for the RNA. He had qualified from Guy's Hospital (MRCS, LRCP) in 1933. (*See*: Anonymous. Iles, Howard Vernon D'Arcy. *Medical Directory 1970*: 1267.)
2. 'Jimmy' and Heather Large were near neighbours of my parents, at East Dean, Eastbourne, West Sussex.
3. A Kirk-Greene. Decorated houses of Zaria. *Nigeria Mag* 1961 (March): 53-78.
4. D Owoyele. Kaduna – administrative town. *Nigeria Mag* 1961 (December): 306-20.
5. **Hugh Waddell Mulligan** CMG qualified (MB, ChB) from Aberdeen University in 1923, and in 1930 obtained the MD. He rose to the rank of Colonel in the Indian Medical Service (IMS), and was successively Director of the Indian Pasteur Institute and the Research Institute at Kasaali. In 1961, he was the Director of the West African Institute for Trypanosomiasis Research at Kaduna. (*See*: Anonymous. *Medical Directory 1960*: London: J & A Churchill: 1651.)
6. V Jones, Pioneer of northern education. *Nigeria Mag* 1962 (June): 26-34; W K R Hallam. In the footsteps of the Shehu. *Ibid* 1963 (September): 196-206; O Nzekwu. From Maiduguri to Lake Chad. *Ibid* 1963 (December): 234-47; O Nzekwa. Banda: the secret of Ibo concentration in Maiduguri. *Ibid*: 248-53.

7. The Sardauna of Sokoto – Alhaji Sir Ahmadu Bello (1909-66) was both the religious (muslim) leader of the north of Nigeria, and Prime Minister of the *northern* region and had been the leading *northern* spokesman during Nigeria's drive for independence. He was also very pro-British, having been educated at Katsina College – on British lines. However, he had little, if anything, in common with the Yorubas and Ibos, and his assassination in 1966 triggered the Biafra War and the humanitarian crisis which went with it (*see* Chapter 1).
8. **Richard Carter** MRCP, MRCPath qualified from Cambridge and St Thomas's Hospital in 1954. He was then a Consultant Pathologist at Birmingham. (*See*: Carter, Richard Alan. Anonymous. *Medical Directory 1970:* 402.)
9. R A Carter, G C Cook. Studies on the serum carotenoids, vitamin A and serum colour in Nigerian soldiers. *British Journal of Nutrition* 1963; 17: 515-22. NB: This was my *first* contribution to the medical literature.
10. Aspiration (needle) liver biopsy was then a relatively newly-introduced procedure when carried out as a routine investigation, although it had a long history. It had been popularised by Sheila Sherlock FRS, with whom I was to work later in my career, at the Royal Postgraduate Hospital Medical School at Hammersmith. I performed many of these procedures both at the Military Hospital, Yaba and the Lagos General Hospital.
11. **Sir James (Wilfred) Cook** FRS (1900-75). (*See*: J M Robertson. James Wilfred Cook. *Biographical Memoirs of Fellows of the Royal Society* 1976; 22: 71-103.)
12. Nsukka is a town in *eastern* Nigeria. Situated about 50 miles north of Enugu, it is the capital of the *eastern* region, and dominated by the Ibo tribe. (*See*: B Ogbuagu. Enugu – coal town. Enugu lies at 600-700 ft above sea level. Coal was first detected there immediately before the Great War (1914-18), and the town rapidly grew up around it. In 1929 Enugu was chosen as the headquarters of the *southern* province, and it presently houses the Government of *Eastern* Nigeria. *Nigeria Mag* 1961 (September): 241-51.)
13. British Army of the Rhine.
14. John Barratt was the landlord of the East Dean public house – 'The Tiger Inn', near Eastbourne (my parents' place of residence).

7

Tour of West Africa: Dahomey, Niger, Togo and Ghana – December 1961

This two-week tour of Dahomey, Niger, Togo and Ghana (see fig 7.1) was undertaken with David Daniels (see figs 7.2 and 7.3), the RNA Dental Surgeon – who had also been seconded during his NS to Nigeria. It took place in early December 1961, and was extremely valuable in providing an in-depth picture of life in *rural* West Africa – well away from the densely populated *urban* city-life of Lagos.

A brief outline of that fortnight is given in Letter 35. Since I did not keep a diary during this trip, I lack details, and my sole reminiscences are outlined in that letter.

I did *not* apparently write any letters *during* the West African tour. Instead, I sent several picture postcards from: Cotonou, Dahomey (now Benin) (8th, 8th and 9th December) with mention of monkeys, hippopotami, parrots and parakeets, and the stilted village (Ganvie) in Dahomey; Togo (three cards, dated 11th December); and Accra, Ghana (two cards, dated 13th December). Those from Dahomey show two groups of male dancers, and a street scene; from Togo, a village scene, and two which are centred on local fishing; and from Ghana, a fishing scene and some typical Ghanaians.

Letter 35 was my last from Nigeria for 1961. Chapter 8 contains the final correspondence of my West African tour – from January to March 1962.

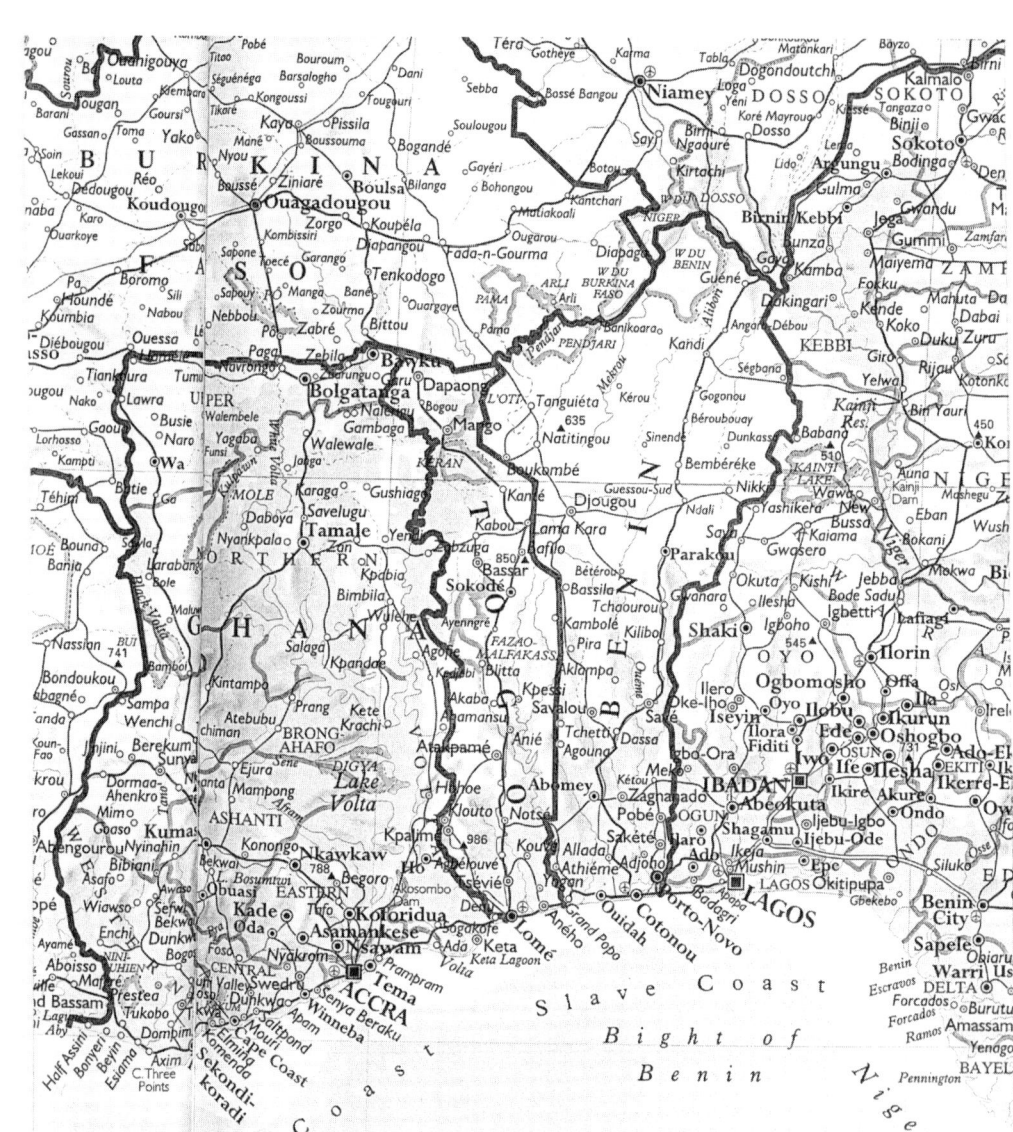

Fig 7.1: Map showing countries of West Africa which were relevant to my December 1961 tour. (Anonymous. Philip's Atlas of the World [in association with The Royal Geographical Society with the Institute of British Geographers]. *London: Octopus Publishing Group Ltd 2006: 262-3.)*

Fig 7.2: David Daniels during the West African tour.

Fig 7.3: Example of a laterite road in West Africa.

Letter 35

Lagos

15th December 1961

[We] have now completed a very memorable trip. The final escape from Kwame Nkrumah [1909-72]'s 'little world' was made ... only just in time – for we had some cash stolen (from the Officers' mess) in Accra & were almost involved with the police, which seems *not* to be a favourable thing in that particular country. The 'political prisons' – old & rather derelict looking castles [these had been used in the slave-trading days – *see* Chapter 1] – did not, one felt appear particularly inviting dwelling places [in which to spend] Christmas.

Kwame Nkrumah was the first president of Ghana, having led the Gold Coast to independence from British colonial rule in 1957. Although founded as a parliamentary democracy, he ruled over an unstable and corrupt regime that saw a steep economic decline, and his underlying concept of African unity was never achieved. In 1966, the army and police force seized power.[1] I continued:

Parts of Accra[2] are very impressive indeed. Black Star Square – with its magnificent arch (mimicking to some extent the Arc de Triomphe in Paris) and at the opposite side, an arch of vast dimensions and of rather contemporary design produce quite a spectacle. Kwame Nkrumah's circle ('circus' to the local European population) – a roundabout of ... vast proportions which is well illuminated at night, is also of note. The Houses of Parliament with Nkrumah's statue [*see* fig 7.4] in the forecourt 'Kwame Nkrumah, the founder of the nation', etc, is also worth seeing.

We visited also the Botanical Gardens – visited by Her Majesty [Queen Elizabeth II – 1926 –present] approx 20 miles N. of Accra – & saw the tree – a young mahogany, which she had planted about one month previously [*see* fig 7.5].

Impressive indeed were the native fishing boats – used in carrying cargo from the ships anchored in the harbour to the shore [*see* fig 7.6]. There are literally scores of these which, pounding their way through the great white breakers of the deep blue tropical sea produce a sight that one will, I feel sure, remember for a long time.

The new university [*see* fig 7.7] – opened two years ago by Prince Philip [1921-present] & which was the scene of a rather unpleasant demonstration

Fig 7.4: Statue of Kwami Nkrumah in central Accra.

Fig 7.5: Mahogany tree planted by HM Queen Elizabeth II in the Accra Botanical Garden.

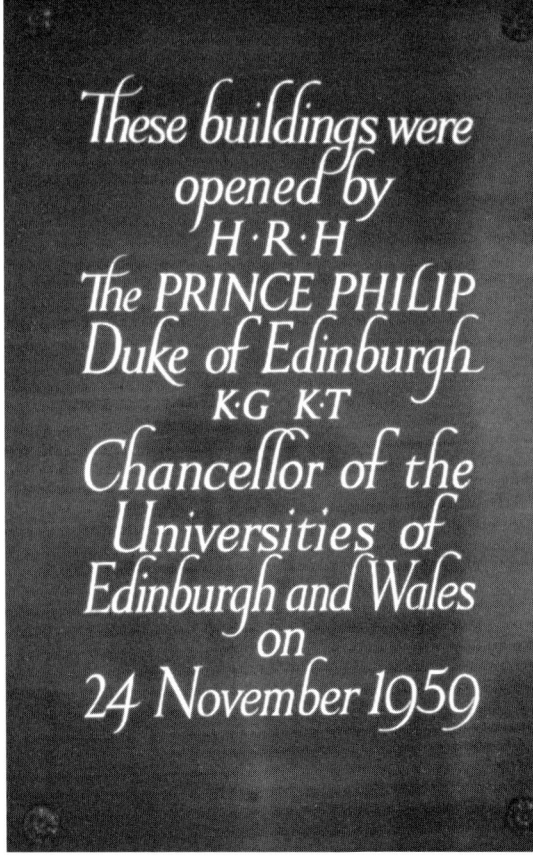

Fig 7.6: Accra, Ghana: canoes in the harbour (one of the few on the West Coast) – used for unloading ships.

Fig 7.7: Plaque commemorating the opening of Accra University in November 1959.

when Nkrumah was installed as Chancellor some few weeks ago, is also a magnificently designed construction.

We were most admirably entertained in the officers' mess by my opposite number in Accra – and in fact I saw the hospital pretty thoroughly – it is approx 2-3 x the size of [the] M.H. [Military Hospital] Lagos – but the medicine is on the whole very similar to that seen here.

That is all I had to say about Ghana. The remainder of that letter concerned our experiences in Dahomey (*now* Benin)[3], Niger and Togo.

So much for Accra, let's go back to the beginning of the trip. The first day was spent at Ibadan – in air conditioned surroundings – quite a luxury here! Then on to Parakou in N. Dahomey; we saw quite a few monkeys that day, playing in the roads and rushing off into the bush as the car approached. Here, as in most of Dahomey, things are still very French. They all speak French, [and] have petit dejeuner, etc, they drink vin rouge ++. In fact if they weren't nearly all black, one might well be in the French countryside.

From here we journeyed to Porga – which was to have been the first [major stop] of our tour, but regrettably, the rest house situated in the midst of the game reserve was closed – so we had to retrace our steps somewhat. The great thing one gathered early on was the vastness of Africa – you can literally motor for 200-300 miles [320-480 km] without seeing scarcely a mud hut, on the most appalling dusty, laterite roads. The temperature – up to 120° [F, or 40°C] at midday and the continual thirst are to be remembered (we took incidentally 10 galls. [45 litres] of reserve petrol, together with 10 gall. water & emergency food supplies, mosquito nets, camp beds etc – for if in fact one was stranded out there it might well be several days before the next vehicle passed by.

Then up to Malanoville at the extreme N-E of Dahomey & across into the Niger Republic[4] – having crossed the great Niger (River). It was here that we saw the hippos. I've some photographs of a rather remarkable sunset over the Niger, which I look forward to seeing. At that level one is almost in the Southern Sahara, & indeed the conditions are very nearly of the desert type – v. minimal vegetation & with incredibly hot days, & nights remarkably cold – in fact I found myself waking up shivering, not with the ague [malaria], but from hypothermia. One sees the rather splendid Hausa horsemen up there and I hope to have some reasonable photographs of one of these [*see* fig 7.8].

At this stage we became somewhat tired of the climate – so hot and dry was it – so instead of continuing across N. Nigeria as we had previously planned, we drove south again [*see* fig 7.9]; in fact over 500 miles between us during the course of one day, to Cotonou – the noted 'seaside resort' of Dahomey [*see* fig 7.10], and what a contrast it was – with its long palm lined beaches, its beautiful deep blue sea and cloudless skies [*see* fig 7.11]. One thing of note near Cotonou is the 'village [Ganvie] on stilts' [*see* fig 7.12] and I've a good many photographs of this also.

On then to Lomé, the capital of Togo.[5] Who'd have thought I'd ever go to Togoland [*see* figs 7.13 and 7.14]. I'd no idea where it was anyway before I came out to the 'West Coast'. A pleasant, rather dozy town – where fishing… palm oil, [and] coconuts etc are the main trades. Quite a pleasant cathedral, but little else, apart from 3 very respectable hotels.

Then to Accra, and I've told you about that – then finally the 330 mile drive home to Lagos yesterday – having completed approx 2,200 miles. Perhaps not a great distance, but enough we felt in these conditions.

And now 10 days to Christmas [*see* Letter 36].

… I suspect that James [my paternal uncle] will go to Nsukka via Kano & Enugu. I will however keep an eye open for him in Lagos, for I suspect he will stay at the Federal Palace Hotel should he come to these parts.

Your weather sounds to be pretty awful, from all accounts. I'm afraid it's impossible here to imagine the cold frosty mornings any more. How fortunate I am in missing your winter in its entirety. …

Fig 7.8: Hausa horseman in northern Dahomey (now Benin).

Fig 7.9: Tribal dancers in a village in Dahomey.

Fig 7.10: The cathedral at Cotonou, Dahomey.

Fig 7.11: Coastal scene in Dahomey.

Fig 7.12: Village (Ganvie) with a population of 10,000 built entirely on stilts in southern Dahomey.

Fig 7.13: Village scene in Togo*.

Fig 7.14: Beach scene at Lomé, the capital of Togo*.

References and notes

1. K Nkrumah. *Ghana: the Autobiography of Kwami Nkrumah.* New York: International Publishers 1971: 310; J D Mahama. *My First Coup d'etat: Memories from the Lost Decades of Africa.* London: Bloomsbury 2012: 318.
2. Capital city of *Ghana* (*see* Chapter 2).
3. *Dahomey* (*now* the Republic of Benin) is an old French colonial possession. Although independent since 1960, French is the language most widely spoken. Dahomey (*see* fig 7.1) occupies some 112,621 sq km of West Africa, the capital city being Cotonou (officially Porto-Novo). In 1625, the Dahomey or Fou tribes established the Abomey kingdom in the south, French forts were built later in the century, and during the *eighteenth* century the kingdom was expanded to include Allada and Ouidah. In

1894, Dahomey became a French protectorate, and ten years later it was incorporated into the federation of French West Africa. Dahomey became independent in 1960, and in 1975 was renamed Benin. The population contains members of the Fou, Yoruba and Fulani – the former being the dominant tribe. There is a hilly region in the north-east, plains in the east and north, and a marshy region in the south. The economy is based on agriculture, and the country has an offshore oil field. An article in the *Nigeria Magazine* contains reference with a photograph of Ganvie, a town with a population of 10,000 which is built entirely on stilts. (*See*: Anonymous. *Britannica Concise Encyclopedia*. London: Encyclopedia Britannica, Inc. 2002: 195; Anonymous. Dahomey – our next door neighbour. *Nigeria Mag* 1961 [September]: 225-40.)

4. The *Niger Republic* (*see* fig 7.1) consists very largely of desert. An old French possession (like Dahomey), it too became an independent state in 1960. Niger lies on the southern border of the Sahara and occupies an area of 188,999 sq km, the capital city being Niamey. There is evidence of a Neolithic culture, and of several pre-colonial kingdoms. Niger became part of French West Africa in 1904, and an overseas territory of France in 1946. Over 50% of the population is Hausa. There is savannah in the south (where most of the population lives), and desert in the centre and north. The south-west is dominated by the Niger river, and the northern-central part is mountainous. The economy is based on agriculture and mining. (*See*: Anonymous. *Britannica Concise Encyclopedia*. London: Encyclopedia Britannica, Inc 2002: 1327.)

5. *Togo* (today, the Republic of Togo) (*see* fig 7.1), which by 1961 was an independent state, had formerly been Togoland, a German colonial possession. It is a country occupying 56,785 sq km, the capital city of which is Lomé. In 1884 it became part of the Togoland German protectorate (previously an intermediate zone between Ashanti and Dahomey). Following occupation by British and French forces in 1914, the League of Nations assigned the *eastern* part of the country to France, and the *western* portion to Britain. In 1946, the country was granted United Nations trusteeship, and ten years later the British section joined the Gold Coast (later Ghana), while the French sector became an autonomous republic within the French Union. The country was granted independence in 1960. Togo contains some thirty ethnic groups, of which the Ewe is the largest. There is a swampy coastal plain, a *northern* area of savannah, and a central mountain range. The economy is mainly agricultural

(cotton, coffee, cocoa, cassava and copra); it is also a leading producer of phosphates, and cement and petroleum refining are also important. (*See*: Anonymous. *Britannica Concise Encyclopedia.* London: Encyclopedia Britannica, Inc. 2002: 1873; Anonymous. Togo: an African Switzerland. *Nigeria Mag* 1962 (March): 45-57.)

8

Lagos, Nigeria
January–March 1962

The final period of my NS days in West Africa began in January 1962. As becomes abundantly clear from my correspondence during these three months, the fascination of this 'foreign' environment had by this time evaporated, and I was clearly looking forward to civilian life again. Local medicine men (or 'witch doctors'), to whom I have not previously referred, had of course been around throughout my tour. However, they did not in any way distract from my orthodox medical work and had certainly 'kept their distance'.

Letter 36

Lagos 2/1/62

… Christmas was very well spent indeed – [I carried out a] Father Christmas act, carved [a] turkey, [and] read one of the 9 lessons [at the Yaba Anglican church] etc. [I] had lunch with one of the better Army families here & dinner with one of my medical colleagues. The great thing here is that you only have to cross the lagoon and you've miles of palm lined beach where you can peacefully lie whilst in [a] hangoverish condition. A whole run of dinner parties of course ensued after Christmas & is still continuing.

Your weather sounds dreadfully cold – in fact the coldest for some time I believe. The whole concept of snow and ice seems too absurd to be true here you know!

Well 3/12 to go I hope – then civilian medicine once again.

I haven't seen the New Year honours list [*see* Chapter 2] yet – [I] shall look forward to receiving yesterday's '*Times*'.

Much of the UK mail has been somewhat delayed of late [due to] Christmas posting I suppose!

[I] was introduced to skin diving on New Year's Eve – a fascinating pastime. [I am] considering purchasing the tackle. …

I seem to have relied more on postcards rather than letters as a means of communication (although I had little to say) during my last three months in Lagos. A card, dated 2nd January, shows a West African village, one of 5th January a couple of Nigerian fishermen, and two dated 10th January, Bornu Warriors from the north, and a fishing scene. A card dated 13th January depicts several Lagos scenes.

Letter 37

Military Hospital

Lagos

21/1/62

Very many thanks for … the local newspaper which I found of great interest. [I] hope the recent numbers of *Nigeria Magazine*[1] have arrived.

Life continues in much the same vein. [I have] just completed a fairly hectic weekend. On Friday I attended the passing out ceremony at the Lagos Police College – and a most colourful ceremony it was – the Sardauna of Sokoto [*see* Chapters 1 and 6] – the leading political figure in Nigeria, apart from the premier, took the salute and the Prime Minister Alhaji Sir Abubakar Tafawa Balewa was sitting just in front of me – quite a spectacle.

On Saturday, the Colonel in Chief of the Royal Nigerian Army, General Sir Lashmar Whistler [1898-1963][2], inspected the hospital and I showed him around my ward etc; and in the afternoon I captained an Army cricket [team] against the Police, led by Sir Kerr Bovell [1913-73][3] – whom incidentally we entertained in the mess following the match. Sunday was somewhat quieter – a day [of] swimming and surfing at Tarkwa bay – and ending [with] a drinks session at one of my fellow officer's houses.

Weather continues [to be] pretty warm.

I gather that your weather has improved somewhat – in fact one of the chaps who flew back from London yesterday was just saying how warm it was!

Yes indeed, the *Practitioners* are arriving satisfactorily; likewise the rest of the mail. I would think that mid-February will be the deadline for sea mail – otherwise it will get lost at this end following my departure – only just over 2/12 left! ...

A card dated 26th January shows a view across the Lagos lagoon, and two dated 30th January, depicts Fulani traders and the Anglican Cathedral in Lagos [*see* Chapter 3]. Cards dated 6th and 19th February 1962 show the Federal Palace Hotel, and Ikoyi Park, Lagos, respectively. My only significant comments on these relate to a forthcoming visit of African heads of state, and of 'an interesting morning in the coroner's court'; this was oriented around a case of suspected poisoning (by ingestion of a corrosive substance – see fig 8.1), and I well remember being asked whether I wanted to take a Christian or Muslim oath! I chose the former. I had attended as the RNA's pathologist (*see* Chapter 5).

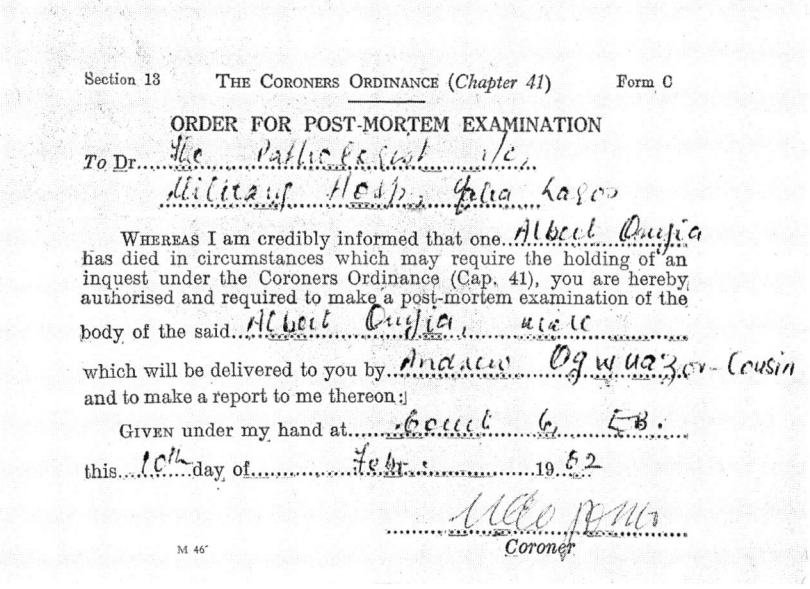

Fig 8.1 Official request for a post-mortem examination (subsequently carried out by me) on the body of Albert Ouija.

Letter 38

Lagos

12th February 1962

… I should think the [final] dates for posting to me in Nigeria should be:-

    {Sea mail   24/2/62

    {Air mail   24/3/62.

I am due to leave on 2/4/62 and arrive in London (as I think I told you previously) on 23/4/62. I have notified 'The *Lancet*' so this journal will be sent to East Dean after 28/2/62.

We've had a cooler spell recently. The Harmattan has been blowing for the past 1/52 – bringing with it the dust and sand of the Sahara, and in fact the night temp has been down to the 60s [Fahrenheit].

… Quite a sprinkling of dinners and cocktail parties again. [I] have made a few social contacts out here! Fairly hectic Mess Dinner last Friday – when the old place became flooded – much to the older members dismay!

… Your postal situation sounds rather difficult. I must say I've noticed no delay in any of the U.K. mail of late, however. …

  A card dated 26th February is of a Nigerian soldier, and a further two (both dated 28th February) show a palm tree and several Hausa horsemen, respectively.

Letter 39

Lagos 7/3/62

… You've kept me pretty well informed of your weather conditions, which sound to be pretty awful. We're still sweltering here, although [we] have had 3 storms during the last fortnight – so it appears that the rainy season may get off to an early start this year.

Spent yesterday a.m. bidding farewell to the G.O.C. – Gen. Foster [*see* Chapter 3] – who entertained us in the ship [the *Apapa*]'s library before he sailed. Jolly good chap; I saw quite a lot of him medically because both he and his wife were ill for short periods during my stay.

I was 'dined out' of the mess on Monday evening, with the Brigadier [*see* below].[4] The R.N.A band [was] present and played throughout the meal, which was pretty fine. After the speeches at these functions, it is then customary to play the various Regimental or Corps marches of the person(s) being dined out – so they gave both the Brig. and myself the baton to conduct these respective tunes! Quite amusing!

The RAMC melody, which I conducted, was 'The Eriskay love lilt' which the Corp's Colonel-in-Chief – HM Queen Elizabeth, the Queen Mother (1900-2002) – favoured.

Saw 2 cases of smallpox[5] [*see* fig 8.2 (a & b)] yesterday [at the isolation hospital], which I had not seen previously, so [I] was quite delighted to have this opportunity [and I] took several photographs.

Smallpox (variola) had formerly (*i.e.* before widespread vaccination) been a serious medical problem in Nigeria, and in 1911 for example, an outbreak of the disease had been fostered by a local 'God of Smallpox' whose devotees disseminated *scabs* from victims of the malady.

One of the other M.O. [Medical Officer]s is being sent home for anti-Nigerian behaviour! So by the time I leave there will only be 2 R.A.M.C. doctors left in Lagos.

Today and tomorrow are public holidays here – to mark the end of Ramadan (the Muslim period of fasting) – 'Id el Fitre'. It's also Ash Wed I believe – Easter is certainly not far off.

… In the very near future I'll have to think about packing I suppose. I've asked the R.A.F. [Royal Air Force] to fly my car home – but this depends upon the availability of space in the '*Hastings*' [aircraft]. …

Two cards dated 12th March show a northerner in ceremonial robes, and a group of muslims, respectively. In one of these, I mention that Brigadier Goulson (*see* above, and who had been 'dined out' with me) had been killed in a car crash. My final letter from Lagos follows:

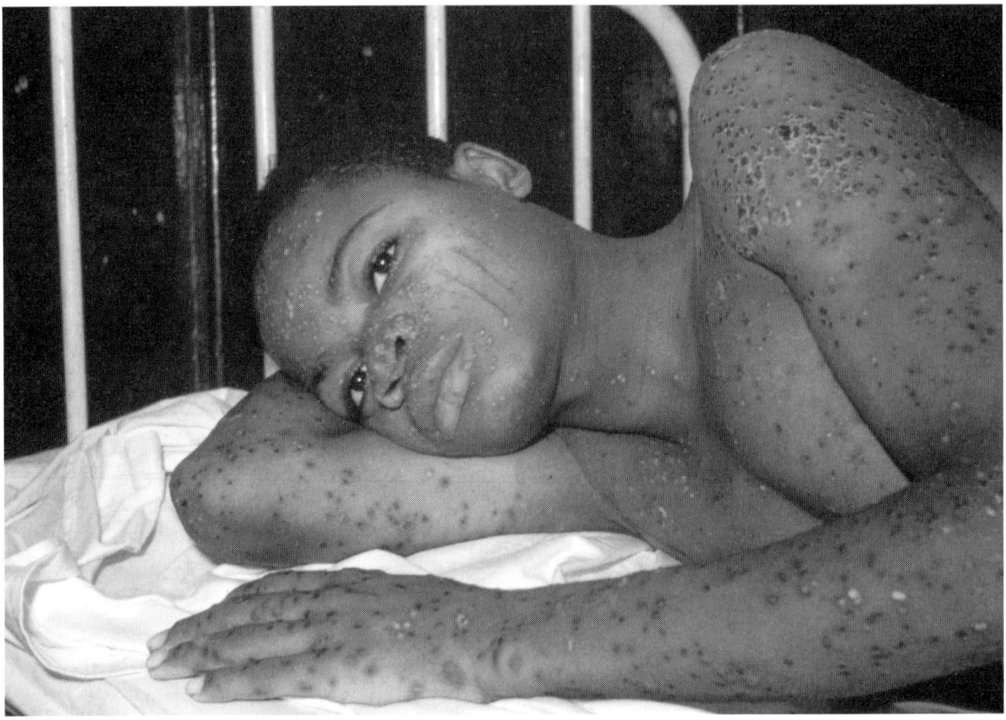

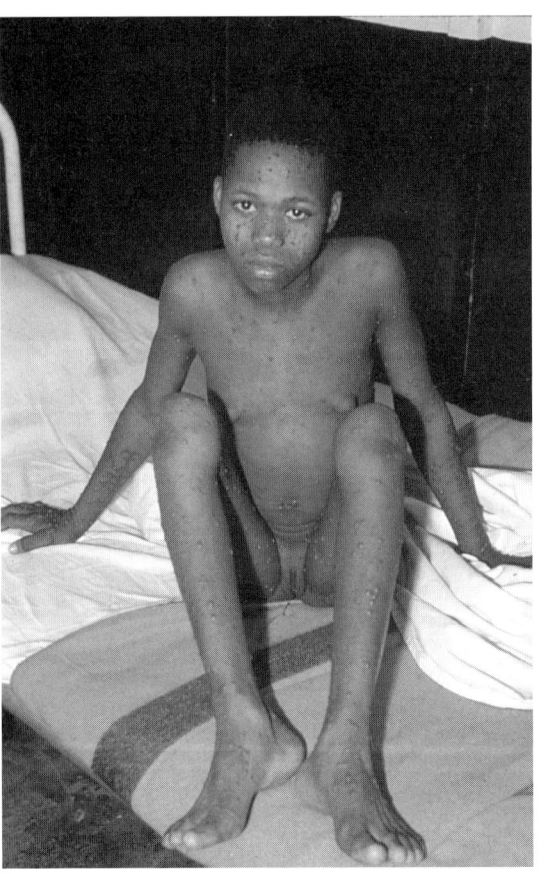

Fig 8.2 (a and b): Cases of smallpox at the Lagos Isolation Hospital.

Letter 40

Lagos

19th March 1962

… I'm now in the depressing position of packing and making the final arrangements for my tour [of the Middle-east]. I shall almost certainly leave Lagos on Sat. 31st March, stay 2 nights at Kano and then proceed to Cairo by Comet (i.e. this is 2 days earlier than previously planned). I shall be holding a fairly sizeable cocktail party on 30th to which I hope most of the Army elite etc will be coming (approx 80 guests I hope).

The weather here has broken up somewhat & in fact a storm takes place most evenings. Accompanying these are frequent power cuts – so I'm getting out I fancy at the right time.

Re my 'Dauphine' – I think I shall manage to persuade the R.A.F. to fly it – although this is in doubt until the last moment. Likewise my cases! …

PS: I am now Commanding Officer of [the] M.H. [Military Hospital] until I leave.

In my final cards from Lagos (24th and 29th March) (which depict a Yoruba woman, and Broad Street, Lagos), I mention a cocktail party at State House – at which I met both 'Zik' and the Prime Minister. I also acknowledged news of the death of my paternal grandmother; Frances (Fanny) Cook, née Wall who had been born on 17th July 1873 at Kimbolton, Herefordshire, and died on 25th March 1962.[6]

References and notes

1. *Nigeria Mag* 1961 (September); 70: 195-294. This issue contained articles on Kwali, the Ejigbo festival, three Nigerian novelists, and Enugu, Ilorin and Dahomey. The following issue (1961 [December]; 71: 295-386), completed the volume and contained articles on Kaduna, Benin art, and Senegal; there was also a review of a book on *Mary Kingsley in West Africa*.

2. **General Sir Lashmar Whistler** was educated at Harrow and the Royal Military Academy, Sandhurst. After a distinguished career in the British Army, he became Colonel in Chief of the Royal Nigerian Army. (*See*: Anonymous. Whistler, General Sir Lashmar (Gordon). *Who Was Who, 1961-1970*: 1192.)
3. **Sir Kerr Bovell** was educated at Bradfield College and had had a distinguished career in various colonial police forces. He latterly became Bursar of Worksop and Radley Colleges. (*See*: Anonymous. Bovell, Sir [Conrad Swire] Kerr. *Who Was Who, 1971-1980:* 85.)
4. **Brigadier Stanley Goulson** had served all of his career in the British Army. He was killed in a car crash later in March 1962 *en route* from Enugu to Lagos. His funeral took place at Ibadan.
5. Smallpox (vaccinia) in 1961 remained an unusual viral disease in Nigeria and elsewhere in the tropics, but with a significant mortality. (H H Scott. *A History of Tropical Medicine* Vol 1. London: Edward Arnold & Co 1939; 648; B Maegraith. *Exotic Diseases in Practice.* London*:* William Heinemann Medical Books Ltd 1965: 361). It had been potentially preventable since 1796, when Edward Jenner (1749-1823) introduced widespread vaccination; however, by no means all Nigerians had been vaccinated. It was not until October 1977 that the last case of the naturally occurring disease was recorded in Somalia. The world-wide eradication programme was organised by the World Health Organisation (WHO). (See: T F McNair Scott. A review of smallpox vaccination from 1774-1973. *Int Dis Rev* 1974; 3: 89-103; A M Behbehani. The smallpox story: life and death of an old disease. *Microbiol Rev* 1983; 47: 455-509; F Fenner, D A Henderson, I Arita, Z Ježek, I D Ladnyi. *Smallpox and its Eradication.* Geneva: World Health Organisation 1988: 1460; G C Cook. The smallpox saga and the origin(s) of vaccination. *J R Soc Hlth* 1996; 116: 253-6.) The other viral disease, which nears extinction is poliomyelitis. (See above: Maegraith; G C Cook, A I Zumla [Eds]. *Manson's Tropical Diseases* 22nd ed. London: Saunders/Elsevier 2009: 263, 871.) However, for political reasons, Nigeria seems likely to be one of the last countries for this to occur.
6. *See*: G C Cook. *Torrid Disease: memoirs of a tropical physician in the late twentieth century.* St Albans, Herts: Tropzam 2011: 3-6.

9

Lagos to London

I did not previously know much about the *Middle East*, so this fortnight was also an introduction to a totally unknown and unexplored region. So rapidly do changes occur in that region, however, that the Middle East of 1962 bore very little resemblance to the situation there today.

The first postcard (posted on 1st April) on my return journey was from Kano in *northern* Nigeria (it pictured the Lagos racecourse), where I visited the mosque and Emir's palace. This was followed by three cards from Cairo (3rd, 5th and 5th April), giving a brief account of visits to the pyramids, sphinx, tombs, the Egyptian museum (and Tutankhamen's treasures) etc. These cards depict the Nile Hilton hotel, the Tower, and the Sphinx and Great Pyramids.

Letter 41

Central Hotel, Kano
1/4/62

… Away from Lagos at last! My cocktail party went off very well indeed – approx 75 turned up, from Brigadiers downwards.

I left Ikeja airport Lagos yesterday evening by BOAC 'Britannia' and had a jolly fine send off – approx 70-80 people came to see me off, both Nigerian[s] and European[s] so I was given a very impressive farewell. [I had] a very good flight from Lagos to Kano – approx 700 miles in 2 hrs.

I had an introduction to a chap in Kano who met me from the airport and has devoted most of today giving me a guided tour of the [town]. The mosque is a most impressive place indeed – as you'll see [from] my photographs. The Emir's palace is a fine building indeed. [I saw the Emir but didn't meet him!

I also saw the radar station which detected Glenn[1] as he passed over Kano during his space flight.

Tomorrow I am due to fly by United Arab Airlines Comet 4C to Cairo – [an] approx 5 hr journey. Incidentally, I'm insured for £20,000 during this flight (policy with Lloyds Bank, Hampstead).

[It is] still very hot although now approx 1,000 miles [north of the] equator. [I also] saw [a] camel train this morning – quite fascinating.

[I] leave Cairo for Jerusalem on 6/4, and on to Beirut on 10/4/62.

[I] will let you have further details of [the] tour later. …

Letter 42

Shepherd Hotel

Mount of Olives Road

Telephone 305

Jerusalem, Jordan

9th April 1962

[I am] just coming to the end of a quite delightful stay here in Jerusalem [*see* fig 9.1]. It really is a quaint old city, in parts almost untouched, one would think, since biblical times [Jerusalem was then situated in the Hashemite Kingdom of Jordan].[2] The more important monuments and sites have of course been very much over-commercialised, but this I suppose is understandable.

[I have] also visited Bethlehem and [the] Church of [the] Nativity [*see* fig 9.2], Jericho, Dead Sea, [and] river Jordan. I've taken approx 100 photographs here so hope to have a fairly good record.

I don't think I've yet written of Cairo – with which I was also most impressed [*see* figs 9.3-9.6]. I spent a lot of time in the Egyptian museum [*see* figs 9.7-9.9] [3] there as well of course as exploring [various] tombs, pyramids, etc. Again, I've a pretty good pictorial record, so [I] won't discuss this at length here.

Tomorrow a.m. I'm due to leave for Beirut in a Viscount of Middle East Airways, and from there on to Cyprus on Friday on a similar plane.

Fig 9.1: The Via Dolorosa, Jerusalem in the Hashemite Kingdom of Jordan.

Fig 9.2: Street scene in Bethlehem: the Church of the Holy Nativity is in the background.

Fig 9.3: The main square in Cairo, Egypt. [See also: Anonymous. The secret of the tomb. Times, Lond 2013; Feb 16: 103.]

Fig 9.4: One of the Pyramids, Cairo.

Fig 9.5: The Sphinx, Cairo.

Fig 9.6: Scene at Memphis.

Fig 9.7: Exhibits in the Egyptian Museum at Cairo.

Fig 9.8: From the Tutankhamun collection.

Fig 9.9: Tutankhamun's chair, the Egyptian Museum in Cairo.

I'm booked, by the way, to reach London on Monday 23/4/62 on flight AZ 288 from Rome (a 'Caravelle' of Alitalia airline I think). I should imagine this will reach London by approx 11-00 – 12.00 midday.

Tuesday 10th April. – Beirut, Lebanon [*see* fig 9.10].

Arrived here at approx 10.00 a.m. this morning – another good flight in a Viscount. I'm at the Omar Khayyam Hotel – overlooking the Mediterranean [Sea] which incidentally I'm seeing for the first time. The flight was interesting, principally in that one had an excellent view of the surrounding mountains – all capped with snow (I believe skiing is still going on!).

Incidentally, my flight from Cairo to Jerusalem was of note in that one had an excellent view of the Suez Canal (pretty narrow … from [an altitude of] 17,000 ft), the Gulf of Suez, [the] Gulf of Aquaba etc, as well as obtaining an excellent idea of this barren, rocky land which constitutes the Sinai peninsula.

I'm certainly learning a lot about the Middle East during this short stay, and am rapidly becoming the classic Yankee tourist. Curiously enough, there are hardly any *British* people travelling in these parts. I only saw two other British people in Jerusalem; all of the tourists are very American indeed.

Well, there's a brief sketch of my past few days. …

    I also sent two postcards from Jerusalem (of the Via Dolorosa and the Garden of Gethsemane) dated 9th April. I wrote of visits to Bethlehem, Jericho, the River Jordan and the Dead Sea (in which I swam). Then a card (showing the Mediterranean Sea) from Beirut (11th April) outlining a visit to Baalbeck, the Museum, and the Cedars of Lebanon. The next stop was Nicosia, Cyprus (*see* fig 9.11), and a card of Bellapais Abbey (*see* fig 9.12) dated 17th April recorded visits to the Troodos Mountains and the Military Hospital at Dhekelia; Cyprus was *not* of course partitioned into Turkish and Cypriot sections in 1962. A card from Athens showing the principal buildings (19th April) recorded visits to the Acropolis, Parthenon and a one-day cruise calling at several Greek islands (*see* fig 9.13). My final cards (20th and 21st April) came from the Vatican City (*see* fig 9.14) (depicted) and Rome (*see* fig 9.15) itself (St Peter's Square). My short tour back to England ended via Paris on Easter Monday 1962 (*see* figs 9.16 and 9.17).[4]

Fig 9.10: Beirut, Lebanon and the Mediterranean Sea.

Fig 9.11: View in northern Cyprus.

Fig 9.12: Bellapais Abbey, Northern Cyprus*.

Fig 9.13: The isle of Poros, Greece.

Fig 9.14: The Vatican, Rome, St Peter's and St Peter's Square*.

Fig 9.15: Street scene in Rome.

Fig 9.16: Notre Dame Cathedral, Paris.

Fig 9.17: The Arc de Triomphe, Paris.

References and notes

1. **John Herschel Glenn** Jr (1921 – present) had become the first (United States) astronaut to orbit the earth on 20th February 1962. He had joined the US Marine Corps in 1943 and flew 59 missions during WWII and a further 90 during the Korean War. He retired from the Marine Corps in 1964 to enter politics but was unsuccessful in a bid to become the 1984 Democratic presidential candidate. In October 1998, Glenn returned to space however, on a nine-day mission aboard the space-shuttle *Discovery*.
2. S S Montefiore. *Jerusalem: the Biography*. London: Weidenfeld and Nicolson 2011: 638.
3. C Desroches-Noblecourt. *Life and Death of a Pharoah*. London: Michael Joseph 1963: 312; F Carnarvon. *Carnarvon & Carter*. Highclere Enterprises 2007: 92.
4. G C Cook. *Torrid Disease: Memoirs of a tropical physician in the late twentieth century*. St Albans: Tropzam 2011: 80-1.

10

Epilogue

I had thus made the most of my compulsory two years of National Service (NS) at the British Government's (taxpayers') expense. NS ended in 1962 (exactly fifty years ago), and this unique period in the history of Britain was therefore to terminate shortly after I was demobilised.

I had gained an in-depth insight into Army life both at home and abroad. In many ways I was strongly tempted to 'sign on' and to make the RAMC my future career. However, it was obvious to me that military medicine (especially in England) could be awfully 'humdrum' and would inevitably involve care – of both a *preventive* and *curative* nature – of basically fit army personnel and their families. I thus ultimately decided that it was 'not for me'.

My previous knowledge and experience of *tropical medicine* had been rudimentary in the extreme. I had been 'thrown in at the deep end' in Nigeria and was heavily dependent on that great textbook initiated by Sir Patrick Manson (1844-1922) in 1898, continued by his son-in-law, Sir Philip Manson-Bahr (1881-1966), and his grandson, Clinton Manson-Bahr (1911-96). My experience of tuberculosis at the (Royal) Brompton Hospital had been of very considerable value, and I was to learn that this remained a *very* important disease, not at that time in Britain, but throughout developing countries generally where poverty was the norm. I also gained a great deal of experience in dealing with malaria, schistosomiasis and amoebiasis in Nigerian troops. My knowledge of many *acute* infections – including lobar pneumonia – was also extended. I had witnessed cases of smallpox (variola) – now extinct as a naturally occurring viral disease – and which I had *not* seen before.

I had learned a great deal about West Africa, and Nigeria in particular, during the immediate post-colonial era. This was to lead to many subsequent years in east and central Africa (as well as other *tropical* locations)[1] – which would almost certainly not have taken place in the absence of these two years of compulsory conscription.

Overall, my two years of *National Service* had thus been valuable from a career perspective. My compulsory introduction to *tropical medicine* – which by this 'accident' was to shape my future[2] – had therefore largely justified these two years spent away from my career in civilian medicine.

A few weeks remained following my return from West Africa until I was a 'free' individual again. Most of this time was spent at Millbank (at that time the Headquarters RAMC Mess), and the bulk of this remaining period was occupied renewing old acquaintances, and seeking future (civilian) employment.[3]

References and notes

1. G C Cook. *Torrid disease: memoirs of a tropical physician in the late twentieth century.* St Albans, Hertfordshire: Tropzam 2011: 93-123, 124-31, 143-55.
2. Ibid: 64-84.
3. Ibid: 81.

INDEX

A

Abeokuta 21; 58; 65; *figs 3.31, 3.32*; 68; 104; 108; 109
Accra 16; 18; 30; 31; 127; 130; *fig 7.6*; 133; 134
Acropolis 156
African Steam Ship Company 28; 29
Akan 30
  see also Ashanti
A League of Gentlemen 86
amoebiasis 99; 162
Annett, Dr H E 22
Anti-Slavery Society 21
A Practical Medico-Historical Account of the Western Coast of Africa (James Boyle) 16; 26n
Ashanti 30; 139n
  see also Akan
Atlantic slave trade 11; 14; 19; 27n; 57; 71n; 89
Audu, Dr Ishaya 44; 70n; 113; 120
Azikiwe, Nnamdi xii; xiiin; 15; 44; 45 *fig 3.6*; 70n; 82

B

Badagry 57; 58; 104
Baikie, Dr William Balfour 90
  see also *Narrative of an Exploring Voyage up the Rivers Kwora and Binue*
Balewa, Alhaji Sir Abubakar Tafawa 15; 64; 72n; 142
BAOR
  see British Army of the Rhine
Barnaby Rudge (Dickens) 11
Barth, Heinrich 89; 95n

Battle of Benin 12
Bearcroft, Dr W G C 81
Beecroft, John 10; 41
Benin
  see Dahomey
Benin bronzes 55; 122; *fig 6.12*
Biafran War 15
'blackwater' fever 17
Blair, Anthony 33
Blair, J S G xi; xii; xiiin
Bleak House (Dickens) 11
Bovell, Sir Kerr 142; 148n
Boyd, Dr J S K (later Sir John) 19; 27n
Boyle, Dr James 16; 26n
  see also *A Practical Medico-Historical Account of the Western Coast of Africa*
Bradley, Dr John 92; 96n
British and African Steam Navigation Company 28
British and Foreign Anti-Slavery Society 21
British Army of the Rhine (BAOR) xi; 126n
Bryson, Dr Alexander 17; 25n; 26n
bubonic plague 13
  Yersina pestis 13
Buloms 30
Buxton, Sir Thomas Fowell 89
  see also *The African Slave Trade and its Remedy*

C

Cairo 108; 113; 147; 149; 150; *figs 9.3, 9.4, 9.5, 9.7, 9.9*; 156
Campbell, Benjamin 20

Carter, Sir Gilbert 44
Chamberlain, Joseph 14; 22
Churchill, Sir Winston xi; 94n
Church Missionary Society (CMS) 58
Clarkson, Thomas 20
CMS
   see Church Missionary Society
Cold War xi
Company of Merchants Trading to Africa 13
Cronin, Dr A J 33; 36n
Crowther, Rt Rev Samuel 90

D
Dahomey (now Benin) 57; 68; 74; 118; 120; 127; 133; 134; *figs 7.8, 7.9, 7.10, 7.11, 7.12*; 138n; 139n; 147n
Daniels, Captain David 38; *fig 3.3*; 56; 64; 81; *fig 5.5*; 118; 120; 127; *fig 7.2*
Dempster, John 29
Dickens, Charles 11
Drew, Lieut-General Sir Robert 5; *fig 0.6*; 8n
Duerden, Dennis 55; 70n
Dutton, Dr J E 22
dysentery 16

E
Egan, Michael 35; 72n
Egypt 1; *fig 9.3*
Elder, Alexander 29
Elder-Dempster Shipping Line 29; 31; 32
Elliott, Dr J H 22
ethnic groups in Nigeria
   see Fulani, Hausa, Igbo (Ibo), and Yoruba

F
Finlay, Dr Carlos 18
Foster-Carter, Dr Aylmer 91; 95n
Foster, Major-General Norman 61; 71n; 72n 98; 122; 144
Fox, George 20
Fulani 11; 90; 139; 143

G
Gagarin, Yuri Alekseyevich 100
Garrod, Prof L P 113
Ghana (formerly Gold Coast) 11; 16; 18; 29; 30; 31; 36n; 38; 99; 107; 108; 111n; 118; 120; 127; 130; 133; 138n; 139n
Glenn Jr, John Herschel 150; 161n
Glover, Sir John 41; 55
Gold Coast
   see Ghana
Goldie, Sir George 13; 90
Grasso, Dr Paul 82; 83; 93n
Great Pyramids 149; 150; *fig 9.4*

H
Hampstead General Hospital 1
Harmattan 42; 61; 144
Harveian Society 56
Hausa 11; 13; 101; 133; 139n; 144
Hawkins, Sir John 57
Head, Viscount 94n

I
Ibadan 8n; 18; 21; 42; 58; 59; *fig 3.30*; 64; 65; 70n; 71n; 86; 89; 91; 92; 104; 108; 110n; 118; 133; 148n
Ibo 11; 12; 13; 15; 25n; 125n; 126n
Igbo
   see Ibo
Ilorin 85; 86; 94n; 147n
'Indirect Rule' 12
Industrial Revolution 20; 21–22; 29

J
Jebba 85; 86; *fig 4.16*; 90; 92; 94n
Jerusalem 108; 150; *fig 9.1*; 156; 161n
Jones, Sir Alfred 29; 36n
Jordan 150; *fig 9.1*
ju-ju 12; 14; 74; 93n

K
Kaduna 8n; 90; 100; 101; 104; 108; 113; 118; 119; 120; 121; 125n; 147n

Kano 57; 101; 134; 147; 149; 150
King Edward VIII 13
Kingsley, Mary 12; 147n
Kirk-Greene, A H M xiiin; 25n; 89; 95n; 125n
Kwarteng, K xiii; 13; 25n

L

Ladder of Bones (E Thorp) 25n; 70n; 98
Lady Chatterley's Lover (D H Lawrence) xi
    see also Lawrence, D H
Lady Chatterley trial xiiin
    see also Lawrence, D H
Lagos Executive Development Board 13
Laird, Macgregor 90
Lambert, Lt-Col Charles 101; 108; 111n
Lancet 85; 144
Lander, Richard 9; 86; 89; *fig 4.15*; 94n; 95n
Laveran, Dr Alphonse 17
Lawrence, D H xi
Leptospira icterohaemorrhagiae 18
Lincoln, Abraham 21
Liverpool School of Tropical Medicine 22; 23; 27n
lobar pneumonia 61; 162
Lokoja (Nigeria) 9; 10; 11; 25n; 72n; 90; 95n
London Gazette 102; 110n
London School of Tropical Medicine (LSTM) 22; 27n
Low, Dr George Carmichael 5; 8n
LSTM
    see London School of Tropical Medicine
Lugard, Lord Frederick 12; 13; 15; 25n; 41; 90
Lumumba, Patrice 61; 72n

M

MacDonald, Sir Claude 12
MacGregor, Sir William 13; 25n; 42
Macintyre, Ben xii; xiiin; 72n
Macmillan Diaries II (ed Peter Catterall) xiiin; 72n; 93n; 110n
    see also Macmillan, Harold
Macmillan, Harold xi; 93n
    see also *Macmillan Diaries II*
Madeira 29–30; 31; *fig 2.1*; 32; 33; 36n
malaria 13; 16; 17; 18; 19; 23; 26n; 27n; 34; 37; 38; 90; 102; 133; 162
    mosquitoes of genus *Anopheles* 23
    P falciparum 17
    Plasmodium spp infection 17
manilla 20; 73; 74
Manson-Bahr, Dr Clinton 162
Manson-Bahr, Sir Philip 27n; 65; 72n; 162
Manson, Sir Patrick 22; 27n; 162
Manson's Tropical Diseases (ed Sir Philip Manson-Bahr) 26n; 65; 72n; 83; 110n; 148n
    see also Manson-Bahr, Sir Philip
McCoskry, William 55
Medical Directory 26n; 63; 70n; 86; 93n; 94n; 95n; 110n; 111n; 125n; 126n
Mende 30
Middle East 1; 147; 149; 150; 156
Millbank 1; *fig 0.2*; *fig 0.3*; *fig 0.4*; 163
More, Kenneth 33
Mossi 30
Murray-Lyon, Dr Ranald Malcolm 19; 26n; 27n

N

Narrative of an Exploring Voyage up the Rivers Kwora and Binue (William Balfour Baikie) 90
National African Company 41; 90
National Service Act 1948 xi
Niger 127; 133; 139n
Niger Coast Protectorate 12; 14
Nigeria Magazine 25n; 55; 58; 83; 94n; 95n 103; 110n; 139n; 140n; 142; 147n; 164n
Nkrumah, Kwame 30–31; 107; 108; *fig 7.4*; 130; 133; 138n
Noguchi, Dr Hideyo 18
Nok culture 11

O
Odoma of Ishara 68; 72n; 74
'Oil Rivers' 9; 16
Ojukwu, C M 15; 25n
Osler Club 56

P
Paludrine
    see proguanil
Park, Mungo 86; 89; 94n; 95n
Parthenon 156
Petraza, Howard 16; 95n
'Philanthropic Experiment' 89
Pope Gregory XVI 21
Povey, Dr John Sullivan 83; 94n
Practitioner 56; 85; 102; 143
Prince Albert 89
Prince Henry of Portugal 11
proguanil ('Paludrine') 17; 38

Q
Quakers 20; 21
    see also Fox, George
Queen Elizabeth II ixn; 130
Queen Elizabeth, the Queen Mother 145
quinine 17; 18; 26; 42; 90

R
Ramadan 64; 145
RAMC
    see Royal Army Medical Corps
Red Cross 61
Reed, Major Walter 18
Reeve, Dr Jeanne 91; 95n
Regulars xi
    see also Reserves
Reserves xi
    see also Regulars
Richardson, Major Stanley 68; 74
RNA
    see Royal Nigerian Army
Robertson, Sir James xii; xiiin; 126n
Robson, Sir Kenneth 91; 95n
Ross, Sir Ronald 17; 26n; 42
Royal Africa Company 13; 19
Royal Army Dental Corps 38; 70n
Royal Army Medical Corps (RAMC) 1; *fig 0.2*; 8n; *fig 0.3*; *fig 0.4*; 9; 26n; 27n; 70n; 122; 125n; 145; 162; 163
Royal Brompton Hospital 1; 44; 95n; 120; 162
Royal College of Physicians (and MRCP) 4–5; 91; 95n; 102
Royal Free Hospital 1; 65; 91; 93n; 94n; 95n
Royal Herbert Hospital 1; 69; 92; 96n
Royal Niger Company 10; 11; 12; 13; 14; 41; 90
Royal Nigerian Army (RNA) 5; 9; 38; 44; 61; 71; 92; 95n; 98; 100; 118; 119; 120; 125n; 142; 148n
Royal Nigerian Navy 100
Royal Northern Hospital 1
Royal Society of Tropical Medicine and Hygiene 83; 93
Royal West African Frontier Force (RWAFF) 5; 44; 90; 121; 164
RWAFF
    see Royal West African Frontier Force

S
Sardauna of Sokoto 15; 126n; 142
Saturday Night and Sunday Morning 100
schistosomiasis 61; 162
Scott, Sir Harold 14; 25n; 164n
Seamen's Hospital Society (SHS) 8n; 20; 22; 27n
Sharp, Granville 20
Shaw, Flora 13
shigellosis 27n; 99n
Sierra Leone 16; 17; 21; 25n; 26n; 29; 30; 32; 36n; 56; 81
SHS
    see Seamen's Hospital Society
sickle-cell disease 19
slave trade 9; 10; 11; 12; 13; 14; 16–17; 19–22; 27n; 28; 30; 36n; 41; 55; 57; 65; 71n; 89; 90 *fig 5.3*; 130
    abolition of 21; 57
    opposition to 20–21; 89

Slessor, Mary 13
smallpox 145; *fig 8.2*; 148n; 162
    variola 162
Society of Friends
    see Quakers
Sphinx 149; *fig 9.5*
SS *Calabar* 28; 30; 35; 37; 59; 61; 64; 72n
Stokes, Dr Adrian 18; 26n

T
Temme 30
Territorial Army 102
The African Slave Trade and its Remedy (Thomas Fowell Buxton) 89
The Citadel (A J Cronin) 33; 36n
    synopsis 34
The Conscript Doctors: Memories of National Service (J S G Blair (ed)) xi; xiiin
The Devil's General 100
Theiler, Dr Max 19
Thorp, E 13; 16; 21; 25n; 27n; 70n; 71n; 73
Times xiiin; 25n; 36n; 70n; 71n; 72n; 94n; 110n; 142
Togo 127; 133; 134; *figs 7.13, 7.14*; 139n; 140n
tropical medicine 1; 5; 20; 22; 69; 73; 162; 163
    see also Blair, J S G
trypanosomiasis 19; 118
tuberculosis 34; 61; 162
Tutankhamun 149; *fig 9.8*; *fig 9.9*

U
UN
    see United Nations
United Africa Company 13
United Nations (UN) 30; 96n; 139
University College Hospital, Ibadan 59; *fig 3.3*; 65; 89; 91; 104; 108

V
Vaughan Williams, Ralph 1; 8n
voodoo 74

W
Webster, J B 58; 71n
Weil's disease 18
Wesley, Rev John 65; 72n
West Africa Council for Medical Research 44
West Africa Council for Medical Research Laboratories 81
West African Medical Service 22
Whistler, Sir Lashmar 142; 148n
'white man's grave' 9–23; 29; 102
Wilberforce, William 20
Winterbottom, Dr Thomas 16; 25n
witch doctors 57; 141

Y
yellow fever 16; 17; 18–19; 26n; 81; 102
yellow jack
    see yellow fever
Yoruba 11; 12; 13; 15; 41; 44; 59; 90; 126; 139

Z
Zarco, Joño Gonçalves 29